WHAT to say or do

IF YOUR CHILD ...

A Parent's Quick Reference for Handling
Common Behavior Problems

JOHNSON INSTITUTE®

What to Say or Do If Your Child...
A Parent's Quick Reference for Handling Common Behavior Problems

Johnson Institute-QVS, Inc.
7205 Ohms Lane
Minneapolis, MN 55439-2159
E-mail: info@johnsoninstitute.com
http://www.johnsoninstitute.com
612/831-1630
800/231-5165

Printed in the United States of America

10   9   8   7   6   5   4   3   2   1

Library of Congress Cataloging-in-Publication Data

What to say or do if your child . . . : a parent's quick reference for
    handling common behavior problems
              p.   cm.
    ISBN 1-56246-147-8 (soft cover)
    1. Discipline of children.   2. Child rearing.
HQ770.4.W477   1998
649'.64--dc21   98-12281
                                                   CIP

TABLE OF CONTENTS

SECTION ONE: AGES 4 TO 7

BEHAVIOR EXAMPLES

- If your child won't brush her teeth

- If your child won't do his chores

- If your child won't fasten his seat belt

WHAT YOU CAN DO

1. Do the task with them, not FOR them.

2. Explain your reasons. For example: "If you brush your teeth, you won't have cavities." Show your child a picture of straight healthy teeth, along with a picture showing a tooth with a hole in it.

3. Have your child repeat the rules back to you, by saying: "I promise to brush my teeth before bed." Reinforce your child by saying: "You've certainly learned to follow these rules well!"

4. Make a list of the rules and post them in your child's bedroom or on the refrigerator. If your child is too young to read, put a picture in the bathroom of a child brushing her teeth.

5. Have your child put a sticker next to a checklist each time he brushes his teeth. Reward each week's progress with a small gift or privilege.

6. Give your child one simple direction at a time. Wait one half-hour before asking her to follow another direction.

7. Make eye contact when giving directions so that you know that you have your child's attention.

8. When giving your child directions, attach a clear time frame to each task. Use a timer so that your child can hear when the time is up.

9. Give your child a few different choices of age-appropriate tasks. Let him pick one or two that he promises to complete. For example, let your child choose between feeding the kitty, folding the towels, or putting the books back on the bookshelf.

10. Let your child know how much her contribution helps. Every child, whether age seven or seventeen, has an important role in helping the home run smoothly and should be complimented for effort.

Don't say: "If you don't do what I tell you, I'll…" Never threaten. Simply repeat your directions firmly and calmly.

DON'T SAY

Do say: Please and thank you.

DO SAY

Make it clear that your child won't be allowed to do anything else until directions have been followed. For example, say, "You will be able to watch your television show once you've put away your toys." If this isn't effective, take away a related privilege. For instance, tell your child, "If you don't put your toys away I will take them away and you will not be allowed to play with them until tomorrow."

SUGGESTED CONSEQUENCES

Children this age should be given clear expectations with specific consequences for failing to follow directions. If your child continues to ignore directions, use a brief time-out (five to twenty minutes alone in his bedroom, depending on your child's age) until he is ready to cooperate.

IF YOU ENCOUNTER SERIOUS RESISTANCE

Teaching my child to follow directions is important preparation for learning to respect authority as he enters school.

PARENT'S AFFIRMATION

SMART TIP

Don't allow your child to buy time in following directions. It's easy to get hooked into "I'll do it in a minute," which often turns into ten minutes, an hour, or never. Procrastination is a manipulation. Insist that your child follow directions immediately when they are given.

② IF YOUR CHILD DOESN'T TAKE CARE OF HIS BELONGINGS

BEHAVIOR EXAMPLES

- If your child is careless with her toys

- If your child throws his clothes on the floor

- If your child damages books or writes on the wall

WHAT YOU CAN DO

1. Show your child how her special objects are to be treated.

2. Explain why it's important to care for belongings. Say, "If you put your book on the bookshelf you'll know where to find it."

3. Create an orderly environment in which there are specific places where your child's belongings should be kept.

4. Have your child save up to buy something he really wants. Anything your child has to "work" for, whether it's by doing some small task or saving his pennies will provide a sense of ownership and teach the value of money.

5. Set a good example by taking good care of your belongings.

6. Put your child in charge of her personal belongings. For example, ask your child: "Where do you think the best place is to put your socks when they're dirty?"

7. Have your child label his belongings with a piece of tape. This reinforces the fact that he needs to be responsible for them.

8. Before bed each night, make sure your child puts her belongings in their proper place.

9. Have your child choose a special toy or other belonging to bring for show and tell. Sharing a favorite possession will help your child want to take good care of it.

10. Make a "wish list" with your child. Each month that your child demonstrates the ability to care for his belongings, reward your child with one item on the wish list.

Don't say: "You've ruined another thing I've worked hard to get you!"

Do say: "When you take care of your belongings, you know where to find them and will have them for a long time."

If your child continually mistreats her belongings, take them away for a period of time. Tell your child that she will get her favorite toy back when she takes care of the others properly. Let her know the consequences ahead of time.

Have your child work to replace objects that have been broken or mistreated. A four year old can earn quarters by helping set the table; a seven year old can take out the garbage or fold the laundry. It doesn't matter whether the job is done perfectly. What counts is that your child makes an effort toward repaying damages.

The earlier I start teaching my child to care for his belongings, the sooner he'll learn a sense of responsibility.

SMART TIP

 Don't automatically replace broken or mistreated objects. Let your child face the consequences of having damaged an important possession.

BEHAVIOR EXAMPLES

- If your child can't sit still at the dinner table

- If your child seems to tune you out

- If your child can't stay focused playing a game or doing an art project

WHAT YOU CAN DO

1. Remove distractions. For example, turn off the TV when you are talking to your child.

2. Keep your child's interest during dinner by engaging him in conversation. For example, "What did you eat for breakfast today?" or "What TV show would you like to watch after dinner is over?"

3. Create a quiet, orderly environment so that your child isn't overly stimulated.

4. Engage your child in short-term activities; for example, a card game that takes no more than five minutes. Then gradually build up to activities that require a longer attention span.

5. Make sure your children are involved in activities that interest them. Sometimes kids this age tune out strictly out of boredom.

6. Let your child know the schedule of events. For example, say, "First we'll be having dinner, then you'll be able to go out and play."

7. Involve your child in physical activity. Let her work off kinetic energy.

8. Give your child short breaks when he becomes distracted, then pick up the activity again.

9. Try to determine if your child is distracted because of fatigue. A short nap can markedly increase attention span.

10. Give your child your undivided attention when interacting with her. Any interruptions, including phone calls, will interfere with her ability to stay on task.

Don't say: "You're not paying attention!"

Do say: "Honey, I'm talking to you," or "Now we're going to . . ."

Create natural cause and effect incentives for improved attention span and allow your child to lose out on them if he isn't making an effort. For example: "You will get dessert only if you finish eating what's on your plate."

SUGGESTED CONSEQUENCES

Seek professional input. Being distracted can be a sign of hyperactivity or attention deficit disorder. In this case, your child shouldn't be disciplined for not being able to control his behavior.

IF YOU ENCOUNTER SERIOUS RESISTANCE

I will work with my child to increase her attention span. If I can't change it through behavior, I will investigate psychological or physiological factors.

PARENT'S AFFIRMATION

SMART TIP

REMEMBER: Effort is what counts. Reward your child, using a star chart or special privileges whenever she makes a clear effort to concentrate.

4 IF YOUR CHILD WON'T TAKE "NO" FOR AN ANSWER

BEHAVIOR EXAMPLES

- If your child argues when you say he can't do something

- If your child keeps pushing and pushing until you give in

- If your child keeps saying "It's not fair."

WHAT YOU CAN DO

1. Decide what is and isn't negotiable. For example, you might be willing to compromise on how much TV your child can watch, but are firm in your convictions about what sort of programming you consider appropriate.

2. Hear your child out. If there's no room for compromise, say: "I understand how you feel, but the answer is still no."

3. Give a simple explanation for your response. You might say: "You can't have a cookie before dinner because it will spoil your appetite."

4. Don't get hooked into extended debates. This is NOT a democracy. If your child continues to argue his point of view, cut it short and say: "This conversation is over."

5. Suggest an alternative when you deny a request, such as: "You can't have a cookie, but you can have an apple or some carrot sticks."

6. Acknowledge your child's feelings of anger and disappointment. Say: "I can see that you feel angry and/or disappointed."

7. If you're not sure where you stand, buy time. Tell your child you'll think about it so that you aren't responding under pressure.

8. Reward your child for not arguing with you. Say: "I really appreciate it when you accept and respect my decision."

9. Teach your child productive ways to express dissent. For example, have her practice saying, "I am unhappy with your decision," or, "I wish you'd give me what I want." Often, expressing disappointment verbally can be empowering even if the answer is still no.

10. Whenever possible, negotiate with your child. For instance, if you say, "You can't stay up past your bedtime tonight," offer an alternative such as, "On Saturday night you can stay up a half-hour later since you don't have to be up in the morning."

Don't say: "I've had enough of this!"

Do say: "We're not talking about this anymore."

DO SAY

If your child persists in arguing, remove yourself from the conversation. Let your child know you're available to talk about other things, but that you will not continue to discuss this any further.

SUGGESTED CONSEQUENCES

If, after saying "no," explaining why, and listening to your child's reasons, she keeps demanding that you change your mind, a time-out is in order. Your child may come out of her room when she is ready to stop pushing. Talk to your child immediately following time-out, by asking, "Are you willing to change your behavior now?" If this isn't effective, seek professional help in order to learn whether your child is acting out due to anger or unmet emotional needs.

IF YOU ENCOUNTER SERIOUS RESISTANCE

It is important for my child to learn that he can't always get what he wants.

PARENT'S AFFIRMATION

SMART TIP

Keep your stress level to a minimum, so that you don't give in because it's the path of least resistance.

5 IF YOUR CHILD GETS INTO THINGS HE SHOULDN'T TOUCH

BEHAVIOR EXAMPLES

- If your child gets into the medicine cabinet

- If your child plays with matches, knives, or power tools

- If your child tampers with harmful household chemical agents

WHAT YOU CAN DO

1. Although it's your responsibility to have all dangerous objects put away, mark all "hands off" items with a "do not touch" sticker as an extra precaution.

2. Eliminate risk by locking anything dangerous in a special cabinet or place that is impossible for your child to get into. This is especially true for tools and guns.

3. Show your child the poison label on products so that she knows that this symbol means "hands off!"

4. Do not leave any dangerous items lying around the house. For example, put matches, knives, medicines, and tools away immediately after using them.

5. Make a list of what your child may and may not touch. Go over the list with your child and post it in a public place in your home. Use pictures for younger children who can't read yet.

6. Give your child safe substitutes to play with. For instance, a Fisher/Price doctor's kit or age-appropriate plastic tool box.

7. Make sure medications have child-proof caps and purchase only child-proof lighters.

8. Be explicit with your child about the serious consequences of getting into things that are off-limits. For example, say: "If you cut yourself with a knife you will bleed," or, "If you swallow these pills you will become very sick and have to go to the hospital."

9. Show your child medications, tools, knives, or other dangerous things around the house and have him explain to you why they're off-limits. One fun way to do this is by having your child present a pretend TV commercial explaining why kids should stay away from these things.

10. Lavishly reward your child whenever she actively chooses to avoid touching or playing with dangerous objects. Say, "I'm so proud that you're smart enough to know what can hurt you."

Don't say: "You'll get in big trouble if I find you touching these things."

Do say: "Never, ever play with these things because you can get badly hurt."

The first time your child gets into something she has been told is off-limits, immediately stop whatever your are doing. Sit your child down and firmly reprimand her, using a very serious tone of voice. If it happens again, temporarily limit her freedom. For example, don't allow her to play outside unsupervised. Tell her, "You will have to stay where I can see you until you show me that I can trust you not to touch that again."

Use scare tactics! If your child continues to ignore your warnings, drive your point home. Show him graphic illustrations: children who accidentally shot themselves, ingested poison, been burned, or hurt by power tools, farm equipment, and other dangerous items.

I will do whatever it takes to keep my child safe.

SMART TIP

Teach your child to call 911 and Poison Control (put the number on your telephone) in case of an emergency. Despite your best efforts, your child may intentionally or accidentally get into something she shouldn't, in which case, have contingency plans in place.

BEHAVIOR EXAMPLES

- If your child kicks and screams when you're trying to get him dressed

- If your child gets hysterical when she doesn't get her way

- If your child has a fit in a public place (shopping malls, the grocery store, etc.)

WHAT YOU CAN DO

1. Remain calm.

2. Do not give in to your child's tantrum. Doing so teaches your child to manipulate in order to get her way.

3. If you are at home, walk away until your child settles down. If you are in public, pick your child up and immediately remove him from the situation. If your child habitually throws tantrums in public, limit his trips to grocery stores, malls, and other places that can create stress.

4. Once your child has calmed down, use role-play, using dolls, stuffed animals, or puppets, to teach your child how to express anger and/or to ask for what she wants.

5. Show your child how to express his feelings appropriately. Use "feelings words" such as "I'm *mad* that I have to go to sleep!" or "I'm *mad* because you won't buy me the toy I want."

6. Create a list with your child of productive ways to express and control anger. Include items such as: Hitting my pillow. Counting to ten. Asking Mom or Dad for a hug.

7. Acknowledge your child's feelings. Say: "I know you're angry right now," or, "I'd be mad too, if . . ."

8. Reward your child for not throwing tantrums. Say: "I'm happy to help you when you ask nicely for what you want," or "Good for you! You should be proud of yourself for handling your anger so well."

9. Be a good role model. Don't scream, threaten, or issue ultimatums when you're angry. Your child will mimic your behavior.

10. Explore tools that might help your child feel more calm and peaceful when she is angry. For example, soothing music, a comfort object (a stuffed animal or blanket), or self-hypnosis (counting backward from twenty) can be useful for regaining composure and self-control.

Don't say: "If you don't stop it, I'll…!" Don't threaten your child or rise to his level of hysteria.

Do say: "As soon as you stop screaming and crying, I'll be happy to help you in any way I can."

Put your child in time-out until she is ready to act appropriately. Give your child a comfort object to help her calm down. Or tell her to "Scream and yell and get all the anger out and then I'll come back and talk with you."

If your child continues to throw tantrums, increase the length of time-outs accordingly and/or take away a favorite toy or privilege. If this doesn't work, a child psychologist can help you explore the roots of your child's anger and frustration.

Learning how to express feelings appropriately is one of the most important life skills I can instill in my child.

SMART TIP

Give yourself some leeway. There are circumstances in which you might choose to pacify your child as a way to avoid an embarrassing scene. Don't worry, it happens to everyone. But try not to let it become a pattern. If you find yourself in this situation, discipline your child as soon as you get home.

7 IF YOUR CHILD PHYSICALLY HURTS OTHER CHILDREN

BEHAVIOR EXAMPLES

- If your child hits other kids

- If your child kicks, bites, or scratches other children

- If your child plays rough on the playground or at school

WHAT YOU CAN DO

1. Explain to your child the natural repercussions of hurting other children. For example, say "No one will want to play with you if you can't play nicely."

2. Intervene immediately if your child causes physical harm. Remove your child and send the other child home if they are playing at your house.

3. If your child isn't attending school yet, supervise all contact with other kids and limit it until your child can conduct herself appropriately.

4. If your child is of school age, notify the school of your child's tendency to kick, hit, bite, or scratch. Ask school officials to call you any time this occurs.

5. Demonstrate nonviolence in your household. Hitting your child teaches her to do the same.

6. Set rules for appropriate behavior, such as no hitting, kicking, scratching, or biting. Have your child make a written or verbal contract such as: "I, Amy, promise to use my words instead of my hands when I am feeling angry or frustrated."

7. Reward your child for consistently following the rules by giving praise or a small gift. You might say, "You should be very proud of how well you handled your feelings by talking instead of hurting."

8. Do not accept ANY excuse for violent behavior. Be sure your child knows it is unacceptable in any and all situations.

9. Provide alternative means of expressing anger physically. Get your child involved in athletic activities, karate, or buy her a punching bag.

10. When your child is physically violent, give him the chance to explain his actions. Be sure to explain that first you will listen, and then your child will need to be quiet and listen to you as well. For example, your child might say, "I had to kick Betsy because she grabbed my toy away from me!" You might respond by saying, "It was wrong for Betsy to take your toy. However, next time, instead of kicking her, come to me or another adult and ask us to help."

Don't say: "Stop acting like an animal."

DON'T SAY

Do say: "It's important to respect other people and not hurt them."

DO SAY

If your child is physically violent toward other children, don't allow him to play with them until he can demonstrate self-control. The message is clear: "When you hurt other people, they don't want to be with you." When your child is in a calm and receptive mood, talk to him about the importance of respecting other peoples' space—especially their bodies—by not hitting, pushing, kicking, or hurting them in any way.

SUGGESTED CONSEQUENCES

If your child can't control her violent behavior, professional assistance may be necessary. Seek advice from teachers, counselors, therapists, or members of the clergy.

IF YOU ENCOUNTER SERIOUS RESISTANCE

Teaching my child alternatives to physical violence at an early age will prevent more serious problems in the future.

PARENT'S AFFIRMATION

SMART TIP

Always have your child apologize if he hurts another child. This is a very effective way of teaching your child to take responsibility for his actions.

BEHAVIOR EXAMPLES

- If your child keeps getting out of bed

- If your child keeps asking for water, hugs, or more bedtime stories

- If your child won't go to sleep unless you stay in the room

WHAT YOU CAN DO

1. Set aside an hour prior to bedtime for stories, cuddling, and backrubs. Give your child your individual attention during this hour.

2. Keep bedtime as consistent as possible. Except for special occasions, decide on a definite bedtime and don't alter it unless absolutely necessary.

3. Create a consistent bedtime ritual (brushing teeth, saying prayers, checking for monsters under the bed) so that your child knows exactly what to expect.

4. Make sure that baby-sitters follow the same ritual.

5. Engage in physical activity with your child in the early evening (playing catch or jumping rope) so that he is tired at bedtime. Try to discourage afternoon naps if possible.

6. Avoid resolving conflicts or arguments with your child right before bed, even if doing so means waiting until morning. Any stressful conversations make it harder for children to fall asleep.

7. Put a night light in your child's room so that she feels safe and secure.

8. If your child gets out of bed once, find out what he needs and then tuck him in again. If it happens again, simply send him back to bed.

9. Lie down with your child or sit in his room for ten or fifteen minutes, then say good night and leave. Unless your child is sick, don't stay in his room any longer.

10. Let your child quietly read a book or listen to a tape until he falls asleep.

Don't say: "I've had enough of this."

Do say: "Please get back in bed right now."

Lack of attention is the best tactic. If your child keeps getting out of bed, stop interacting and responding to his requests. Simply say: "Go back to your bedroom."

SUGGESTED CONSEQUENCES

Try to find out if there's anything serious bothering your child that is keeping her from falling asleep. If there isn't, you may need to impose stricter bedtime rules. Tell her, "If you get out of bed again, you'll be put to bed earlier," or, "I will read you a story only if you stay in bed."

IF YOU ENCOUNTER SERIOUS RESISTANCE

It's important for my child to go to bed and stay in bed so that he will be rested and so that I can have some much-deserved peace and quiet.

PARENT'S AFFIRMATION

SMART TIP

Don't be seduced into extending bedtime because your child says: "I'm scared of the dark," or pleads for "just one more story." Set the rules and stick by them.

9 IF YOUR CHILD IS AFRAID TO GO TO THE DOCTOR, DENTIST, ETC.

BEHAVIOR EXAMPLES

- If your child cries on the way to or during doctor or dental appointments

- If your child is scared of shots

- If your child clings to you and won't let the doctor or dentist examine him or her

WHAT YOU CAN DO

1. Explain to your child ahead of time exactly what is going to happen and how long it will take. If you aren't sure, call the doctor's or dentist's office and ask.

2. Have your child play doctor or dentist, using a plastic stethoscope, thermometer, and other toy medical instruments.

3. Make a "getting acquainted" visit to your child's doctor or dentist so that he can see the office and meet the staff prior to an actual exam.

4. Let your child know it's okay to feel scared. Don't try to talk your child out of her feelings.

5. Explain to your child why it's important to see the doctor and the dentist. For example, say: "It's the doctor's job to help keep you healthy," or "Going to the dentist will make your teeth clean and strong."

6. Remain in the room with your child during the appointments.

7. Hold your child's hand and her that she is being very brave.

8. Let your child bring a comfort object (a stuffed animal or blanket) along to the appointment.

9. Reward your child with a special treat after the appointment; for example, a sticker, toy, or cup of frozen yogurt.

10. Keep a star chart of regular doctor and dentist appointments. Your child can place a new sticker on it each time he has a successful visit. Keep track of your child's height and weight on this chart, too. This will keep him interested in how he is growing.

Don't say: "Be a big boy/girl."

Do say: "Yes, this is scary, but I know you can get through it."

Fears of going to the doctor or dentist shouldn't be viewed as misbehavior, but rather emotional apprehension. This is an area in which reassurance, not discipline, is in order.

If your child develops a phobia about going to the doctor or dentist, make sure that your medical provider is "child-friendly." If you feel confident of this, then your child's fears may be deep-seated and require professional intervention.

I will do everything in my power to help my child feel comfortable and secure during medical appointments.

SMART TIP

Be honest with your child. Never say: "This won't hurt," if it will. Instead say: "This might sting for a minute, but then it will be over." Kids feel betrayed if parents aren't straight with them.

BEHAVIOR EXAMPLES

- If your child demands your attention by poking or tugging at you when you're talking to someone else

- If your child interrupts you when you're on the telephone

- If your child won't let you finish a sentence without breaking in

WHAT YOU CAN DO

1. Firmly say: "I will give you my full attention when I am finished talking to . . ."

2. Set a good example by not interrupting your child or other family members.

3. Involve your child in an activity before you begin an adult conversation.

4. Let your child know when you will be available to respond. For example, say: "In five minutes, I will be off the phone and ready to talk to you."

5. Teach your child to take turns talking. Make it a game, using a stopwatch, in which you and your child each get to say anything you want for two minutes without interruption, then switch.

6. Praise your child for not interrupting. You might say: "Thank you so much for waiting until I was finished."

7. Don't allow your child to interrupt you even if she sulks, cries, or tugs at your arm. Unless it's an emergency, don't tolerate interruptions.

8. Teach your child to say, "Excuse me," when your attention is urgently needed.

9. Agree with your child on what constitutes the need for interruption, for example, finding a bathroom quickly in a public place, something burning on the stove, etc.

10. Role-play with your child in order to illustrate what an interruption is. For example, ask him to tell you about what happened at kindergarten today. Break in so that he understands why it's rude to interrupt.

Don't say: "Stop being rude and interrupting me."

Do say: "Please wait your turn until I am finished."

If your child interrupts more than once for non-urgent reasons, say, "Pardon me, but you are interrupting." Remove yourself from her presence or send your child to her room. This gives your child the opposite of what she really wants, which is your attention.

If your child interrupts even after being repeatedly put in time-out, employ stricter disciplinary measures by removing privileges. Factor in your child's age. A young child can have a favorite toy taken away until he stops interrupting. An older child might lose one or two nights of watching television until he can exhibit more considerate behavior.

Interrupting is rude. Teaching my child not to interrupt is good preparation for learning to wait her turn in school and other social situations.

SMART TIP

Before beginning an adult conversation, ask your child if he needs to talk to you about anything. Make sure your child's needs are met so that you can feel comfortable expecting him to wait.

BEHAVIOR EXAMPLES

- If your child won't let other children touch or play with his toys

- If your child refuses to share food, such as giving another child one of his cookies

- If your child is overly possessive about her belongings and freaks out if a sibling asks to borrow a book or a game

WHAT YOU CAN DO

1. Set a good example by sharing with your child, spouse, or other children.

2. Let your child decide what he is and isn't willing to share. Allowing him to choose one or two precious objects that needn't be shared, along with several that will be shared, gives your child some feeling of control over his belongings.

3. Invite your child's friend to bring a special toy or game and facilitate sharing by having each child take turns with the other's toy.

4. Make sure your child always brings a few of her own things to share when she is playing at another child's home.

5. Explore your child's reasons for refusing to share. He may be afraid that toys will be lost or damaged, or that there aren't enough cookies.

6. Reassure your child that material possessions can be replaced and that there is plenty of food to go around.

7. Explain to your child that refusing to share will make other children unwilling to play with her.

8. Designate certain objects such as food, the television, and certain books and games in your home as "communal property." This will help your child gets used to the concept of sharing.

9. Involve your child in charitable giving by having him help deliver Thanksgiving baskets, do volunteer work (even a five-year-old can visit a nursing home), or put aside a few pennies a week to give to a local charity. Doing this will help increase your child's sense of abundance and feelings of gratitude.

10. Reward your child every time she shares. Use verbal reinforcement such as, "It's terrific that you're letting your friend use your colored pencils." Or give your child a small gift (a new pencil sharpener or sticker). The message is: "The more you share, the more you will have."

Don't say: "Stop being so selfish and spoiled."

Do say: "It's good to share."

After one reminder, take away the item your child won't share and don't give it back until she is ready to try it again.

If you can't get your child to learn to share, employ two more dramatic consequences: Don't allow your child to play with other children until his behavior improves, and don't share with your child. For instance, say: "I'm sorry, but you can't have a bite of my cake," so that your child experiences withholding firsthand.

Teaching my child to share is a fundamental building block to developing healthy relationships with others.

SMART TIP

When your child is generous, take some time to talk with her about how good it feels to share. Help your child discover and express her feelings of satisfaction and pride.

**BEHAVIOR
EXAMPLES**

- If your child whines when she doesn't get what she wants

- If your child whines in order to get attention

- If your child whines when he's bored and can't find anything to do

**WHAT YOU
CAN DO**

1. Don't give in to your child's whining by giving him what he wants.

2. Tape record your child whining and make her listen to it several times.

3. Teach your child how to communicate without whining. Have him practice speaking in a normal tone of voice.

4. Be attentive. Let your child know that you heard her the first time by repeating what she said. For example: "I know that you're bored," or "It sounds as if you're hungry."

5. Put your child in charge of "fixing" his problem. For instance, say, "If you're bored, what would you like to play with right now?" Or, "It sounds like you're hungry. There are apples in the fridge if you want to get yourself one."

6. Remind your child not to whine. Walk out of the room so that he will learn that this isn't the way to get your attention.

7. Make sure that your child isn't whining because she is under the weather.

8. Distract your child from droning on and on by engaging him in a fun and involving activity.

9. Acknowledge your child's anger, frustration, or disappointment by saying, "It's much easier to hear about your feelings when you don't whine."

10. Get earplugs or put on headphones with soothing music until your child has stopped whining. Your child will get the message.

Don't say: "You're giving me a headache."

Do say: "When you stop whining I'll listen to what you have to say."

Once you've established that your child isn't sick or in any danger, ignore her until the whining stops.

Incessant whining should be punished with immediate time-outs, appropriate to your child's age. This behavior also can be a sign of inner frustration which may be best explored with the help of a child psychologist.

I won't allow myself to be worn down by my child's whining. I will consistently insist that she communicate more appropriately.

SMART TIP

Make a positive behavior contract with your child, for example: "I will stop whining. When I have gone two days without whining, I will get to stay up a half-hour later or pick out a special treat at the toy store."

13   IF YOUR CHILD IS SHY AND WON'T INTERACT WITH OTHERS

BEHAVIOR EXAMPLES

- If your child won't play with other children

- If your child stands on the outskirts of the playground and watches

- If your child clings to you in social situations

WHAT YOU CAN DO

1. Invite a playmate to come to your home where your child is comfortable.

2. Don't overwhelm your child with more than one friend at a time. Kids who are shy do better in a one-on-one situation.

3. Stay in the room while your child is playing with her friend. Each time the friend visits, gradually wean your child from your presence. At first, leave the room for short periods. Later move into another part of the house for a longer period of time.

4. Instead of letting your child cling to you or hide behind your back in social settings, firmly hold your child's hand and continue your conversation without apologizing for or making a big deal out of his shyness.

5. Go with your child the first few times she is invited to play elsewhere.

6. Allow your child to be an observer until he is ready to join in.

7. Facilitate nonverbal activities in which your child can participate, such as catch, tag, or playing on swings with another child.

8. Make sure other adults—teachers, baby-sitters, etc.—are aware of your child's shyness so that they will approach her appropriately.

9. Explore the feelings beneath your child's shyness. For example, your child may feel intimidated by grown-ups or worried about gaining his peers' approval. Or perhaps he is scared of new situations or people.

10. Let your child set her own pace. She will engage with others according to her own temperament and comfort level.

Don't say: "There's nothing to be scared of. Now go ahead and play with the other kids."

Do say: "Let's walk over there together and show Susie your new doll."

Your child shouldn't be disciplined for shyness, which is part of his personality rather than misbehavior. You can, however, discuss the natural consequences of shyness. For example, gently remind your child that the only way to make friends is by taking a risk and coming out of his shell.

SUGGESTED CONSEQUENCES

When your child enters school, if she continues to be painfully shy and unable or unwilling to interact with others, this may be a sign of emotional distress or a phobia. This situation is best dealt with by a professional child psychologist.

IF YOU ENCOUNTER SERIOUS RESISTANCE

Every child is different. I will help my child overcome shyness without expecting him to have a more outgoing personality.

PARENT'S AFFIRMATION

SMART TIP

Let your child set the pace. Don't push, just gently encourage her to slowly become more comfortable relating to others.

SECTION TWO: AGES 8 TO 12

1 IF YOUR CHILD "FORGETS" TO DO THINGS

BEHAVIOR EXAMPLES

- If your child "forgets" to straighten up her room

- If your child "forgets" he has homework assignments

- If your child "forgets" to say please and thank you

WHAT YOU CAN DO

1. Immediately remind your child of her responsibilities.

2. Don't accept "forgetfulness" as an excuse.

3. Prepare a daily written list of responsibilities for your child to check off.

4. Review your child's responsibilities with him each morning and night. Be sure to explain to your child how his contributions help make your family and home run more smoothly.

5. Remind your child of her responsibilities ahead of time.

6. Establish regular times and routines for your child to perform his duties.

7. Reduce distractions by turning off the TV or stereo when your child is supposed to be studying or doing other tasks.

8. Assist your child in doing things that she finds difficult or uninteresting.

9. Make eye contact when you remind your child of what he is supposed to do.

10. Try to find out why your child is "forgetting" to do certain things, and discuss the possibility of finding other chores she is more willing to take on.

Don't say: "You'll keep getting punished until you start taking your responsibilities seriously."

Do say: "The more you take responsibility for doing what you're supposed to do, the more freedom and privileges you'll be given."

Do not allow your child to do anything else until he has taken care of what needs to be done. If this behavior continues, gradually remove privileges until your child demonstrates the willingness to "remember" what he needs to do.

If your child chronically "forgets" to do important things, she may need clinical assessment for attention deficit disorder. As a last resort, seek professional help that may enable you to discover behavior strategies for keeping your child on task.

Remembering what needs to be done is a key to assuming responsibility. I will keep working with my child when he "forgets" to take care of his responsibilities.

SMART TIP

Kids, like adults, are more bound to "forget" taking care of things that are either difficult or don't interest them. Try to help your child find fun and creative ways to handle the responsibilities he is avoiding.

2 IF YOUR CHILD BEHAVES INAPPROPRIATELY IN PUBLIC

BEHAVIOR EXAMPLES

- If your child gets into fights at school

- If your child is disorderly in public places, such as on the playground, at shopping malls, or in movie theaters

- If your child is rude to other people, either at home, in public, or at the homes of relatives or friends

WHAT YOU CAN DO

1. Find out why your child feels provoked to the point of anger. If there is a specific child with whom he gets into fights, try to speak with the other child's parent. Or, ask a school counselor to intervene, sit down with the two children together, and use conflict resolution skills.

2. If your child is disorderly in public, immediately remove her from the scene.

3. Limit your child's freedom to be out in public places unless accompanied by parents or another supervising adult.

4. Don't be embarrassed or intimidated by your child's behavior. Stay calm and in charge and if at all possible, remove him from the situation.

5. Discuss the appropriate way to behave in public. Define rudeness by using examples such as interrupting, being aggressive, screaming, yelling, or making a scene. Practice role-playing with your child. For example, demonstrate the correct way to handle potential fights on the playground or how to interact with store clerks and other employees in public places.

6. If your child is rude to others, stop what you're doing. Immediately discipline your child by putting her in time-out or taking away a privilege.

7. Insist that your child apologize any time he is rude or disorderly.

8. Be sure to tell your child that you disapprove of her *behavior*, not that you disapprove of her as a *person*.

9. Make sure your child is rested and not hungry when he goes out in public, whether it's to school or to social occasions.

10. Reinforce your child's appropriate behavior in public with verbal praise. Tell your child, "You really handled that well!" or reward him with increased privileges.

Don't say: "How dare you embarrass me like that?!?"

Do say: "I expect you to behave appropriately in public."

Inappropriate behavior is best dealt with on the spot, using verbal intervention and immediate consequences. It's most effective to take away privileges that are related to the behavior. For example, if your child fights with friends on the playground, she should lose recess privileges. Or, if your child can't handle herself at the mall, she shouldn't be allowed to go there.

SUGGESTED CONSEQUENCES

Most children are motivated to improve inappropriate behavior through loss of privileges. If this isn't effective, your child may have more serious psychological issues underlying his behavior. A skilled family counselor can help you and your child explore anger or frustration that may be contributing to his behavior.

IF YOU ENCOUNTER SERIOUS RESISTANCE

Learning to act appropriately in public is a very important life skill. I will continue to expect my child to behave well in public, and will enforce consequences when she fails to meet these expectations.

PARENT'S AFFIRMATION

SMART TIP

 Don't take it personally. Your child's inability to behave appropriately in public is not a reflection of poor parenting on your part.

3 | IF YOUR CHILD WATCHES TOO MUCH TV

BEHAVIOR EXAMPLES

- If your child watches television when he is supposed to be doing homework
- If your child watches television instead of being engaged in other activities
- If your child watches television programs that you disapprove of

WHAT YOU CAN DO

1. Turn off the TV. Don't allow it to provide background noise during dinner or other family activities.

2. Sit down with your child and define how much television she is allowed to watch.

3. Make watching television a reward for finishing homework and other tasks.

4. Set a specific limit for how much TV your child is allowed to watch on a daily basis.

5. Make sure your child participates in athletic activities and other healthy social outlets instead of passively sitting in front of the TV. Remove the TV from the bedroom to stop your child from lying on his bed and staring at the TV.

6. Be a good role model by limiting how much TV you watch.

7. Create a list of acceptable TV shows. Don't allow your child to watch the shows that have violence or other negative influences. Consult rating systems that can warn you of sexual and violent content.

8. If your child watches shows you disapprove of, take away television privileges until he earns the privilege back.

9. Make a point of doing fun family activities that replace television in the evening or on weekends.

10. Sit down with your child and the TV schedule and plan the shows she wants to watch. Then carefully choose according to the time limits you've set.

Don't say: "Turn off that darn TV!"

Do say: "It's time to turn off the television and focus on other things right now."

Decrease television privileges each time your child fails to follow the rules. Once she demonstrates a respect for the limits, gradually increase the time she is allowed to watch television.

Obsessive television watching can be a sign that your child is bored or withdrawing from the rest of the family. If this behavior continues, make television watching off-limits, and seek professional help to aid your child in developing other, healthier, and more active interests.

I will treat watching television as a privilege, not a habit.

SMART TIP

 Disconnect the television until your child shows that he is capable of respecting the rules. You may be surprised to find how creative your child is in finding other ways to entertain himself.

BEHAVIOR EXAMPLES

- If your child pretends to not hear you when you are speaking to him

- If your child ignores your requests to get ready on time

- If your child ignores your instructions to clean his room, turn off the TV, or complete his tasks

WHAT YOU CAN DO

1. Have your child's hearing checked to make sure there is no medical problem.

2. Speak to your child directly, making eye contact, rather than giving instructions from across the room.

3. Don't accept "I didn't hear you," as an excuse. Let your child know that ignoring you is unacceptable behavior.

4. Remove all distractions when speaking to your child. Turn off music or the television.

5. When you ask your child to do something, have her repeat the instructions back to you so that you know she has understood.

6. If your child ignores you, have him write down your instructions and cross them off the list once they are met.

7. Be sure not to ignore your child, so that she learns that this is inappropriate behavior.

8. Point out the direct consequences of your child ignoring you. For example, if your child ignores your instructions to get ready for bed on time, he will be tired in the morning. Or, if your child ignores his homework, his grades will be affected.

9. Provide positive reinforcement by rewarding your child when she listens.

10. Before entering a public situation, remind your child that he must listen to you, especially for safety reasons. For instance, a child who doesn't stay close to Mom or Dad at the mall may get lost and get into trouble as a result of tuning out.

Don't say: "I'm not going to tell you this again!"

Do say: "I expect you to pay attention when I speak to you."

If your child continues to ignore you, enforce the following consequences: don't allow her to do anything else until she has listened to and responded to your request. If your child persists in ignoring you, take away privileges until this behavior improves.

Sometimes kids act out by ignoring parents as an expression of anger, anxiety, or frustration. In these cases, intervention by a school or family counselor can be useful.

I will insist that my child shows respect by listening to what I say. Being firm and consistent about my expectations will help my child cultivate respect for authority figures.

SMART TIP

Don't get "hooked" into your child ignoring you by becoming angry or threatening. Calmly repeating instructions—and removing privileges as a consequence—is a far more effective strategy.

5 | IF YOUR CHILD PROCRASTINATES

BEHAVIOR EXAMPLES

- If your child waits until the last minute to finish homework assignments

- If your child puts off completing her chores

- If your child is always rushing to be ready for the school bus

WHAT YOU CAN DO

1. Create a work plan with your child outlining his daily responsibilities.

2. Determine how much time each activity (task, homework) will realistically require.

3. Reward your child for finishing tasks on time, with a special treat or privilege, such as an extended bedtime or a small gift.

4. Show your child the positive consequences resulting from completing tasks in a timely fashion. For example, point out how good it feels to have homework finished on time. Or, show how relaxing it is to have an extra fifteen minutes in the morning to eat breakfast and get ready for school instead of rushing.

5. Have your child organize her room and work space so it is easier for her to tackle tasks. Regularly help your child make sure that this space is well-organized and conducive to getting things done.

6. Allow natural consequences for your child's procrastination. For example, friends may not be able to come over because they didn't receive enough advance notice from your child. If homework is suffering due to procrastination, your child will get a lower grade. Limit social and after-school activities so that the priorities are attended to first.

7. Establish a regular routine for your child so that he knows exactly what is expected, in what order, at what pace.

8. Instruct your child to get things done in the present, rather than discussing tasks that need to be done at a later time. This will help your child focus immediately on taking care of what needs to be accomplished.

9. Use a timer to help your child monitor how much time she has to complete a particular task. You can also set clocks ahead fifteen minutes so that your child has extra time and doesn't feel as rushed.

10. Be available to help your child complete tasks that he constantly puts off. If possible, make it a fun, family activity.

Don't say: "You'd better get this done right now, or else."

Do say: "This needs to be done now. Is there anything I can do to help you get it finished on time?

Natural consequences are bound to result from your child's pattern of procrastination. Not finishing homework, putting off chores, or waiting until the last minute to make plans inevitably create negative results, which hopefully will motivate your child to stop procrastinating. You can reinforce these consequences in two ways:
1. Allow natural consequences to occur, without rescuing your child.
2. When there aren't natural consequences, remove privileges when your child procrastinates in order to reinforce the seriousness of this behavior.

SUGGESTED CONSEQUENCES

Procrastination is basically a bad habit which can be improved through natural consequences and parental discipline. However, if these measures don't make a difference, your child's procrastination may be a symptom of perfectionism. Seek help from a child psychologist. Perfectionists may put off completing tasks due to fear of failure.

IF YOU ENCOUNTER SERIOUS RESISTANCE

Real life requires the ability to meet deadlines. I will make a serious effort to help my child stop procrastinating.

PARENT'S AFFIRMATION

SMART TIP

Create an orderly environment and a regular routine. This is more conducive for a child to complete tasks on time.

BEHAVIOR EXAMPLES

- If your child curses, makes obscene gestures, or uses other bad language

- If your child burps, picks his nose, or eats with his mouth open

- If your child interrupts or is verbally aggressive or abusive to others

WHAT YOU CAN DO

1. Discuss what constitutes good manners. Make a list of good manners and post it on the refrigerator where it is highly visible.

2. When your child uses bad manners, immediately correct him or her by saying: "It is bad manners to pick your nose, burp in public, etc. I expect you to act appropriately at all times."

3. When your child uses bad manners in public or toward others, insist that she apologize for her behavior.

4. Teach the importance of good manners. Be a good role model by using good manners yourself so that your children can emulate your behavior.

5. Reinforce good manners by saying, "You should be very proud of what lovely manners you have."

6. When your child exhibits bad manners, limit his social activities. For example, don't allow him to have friends over or attend parties until he demonstrates the ability to be polite.

7. Don't accept the use of any foul or obscene language. Make a list for your child of all unacceptable language and enforce immediate consequences if your child violates the expectations you've set.

8. If your child displays bad manners at the dinner table, send her to her room until she can be a socially acceptable dining companion.

9. Don't criticize your child in front of other people. Take him aside and express your feelings in private.

10. For those public situations in which it is uncomfortable to do so verbally, set up a nonverbal signal with which you can inform your child that she is using bad manners.

Don't say: "Stop embarrassing me!"

DON'T SAY

Do say: "Your bad manners are unacceptable. The way I expect you to behave is ..."

DO SAY

Once kids are given a set of rules for good manners, any violations should be immediately dealt with through disciplinary measures. Use time-out or loss of privileges until your child improves his manners.

SUGGESTED CONSEQUENCES

Depending on your child's age, she may be influenced by negative peer pressure which reinforces her bad manners, especially cursing or using other obscenities. If loss of privileges isn't effective in getting your child to improve her manners, consider whether or not she is hanging out with kids who are a bad influence. Censor certain television shows since kids can also pick up bad manners watching TV, e.g., hearing actors swearing, watching sexually explicit music videos, seeing ballplayers spitting, etc. Check with your child's school counselor to see whether bad manners are also being exhibited at school. If so, consider professional counseling to determine whether underlying anger or frustration are contributing to your child's behavior.

IF YOU ENCOUNTER SERIOUS RESISTANCE

Learning good manners begins in the home. Being gracious and well-mannered is an important life skill that will serve my child as he ventures out into the world.

PARENT'S AFFIRMATION

SMART TIP

Be careful not to laugh or in any way encourage your child's bad manners. Even if it's slightly amusing when your eight year old says a swear word or your twelve year old gives another driver the finger when he cuts in front of you, any inconsistent response will confuse your child and undermine your efforts.

IF YOUR CHILD MAKES EXCUSES FOR HIS BEHAVIOR

BEHAVIOR EXAMPLES

- If your child says he forgot to take care of his responsibilities

- If your child blames others for her mistakes

- If your child acts victimized, saying things like: "I can't help it. It just happened."

WHAT YOU CAN DO

1. Do not accept any excuses for your child's behavior.

2. When your child makes a mistake, calmly discuss what he could have done differently to prevent it.

3. Listen to your child's explanation before assuming she is to blame.

4. Discuss strategies for avoiding similar problems or mistakes in the future.

5. Teach your child to make "I-Statements" such as, "I forgot to turn in my homework," or "I got angry and got into a fight on the playground."

6. Reward your child for taking responsibility for her behavior with verbal praise. For example say, "Good for you for admitting your mistake. I really appreciate it when you are honest."

7. Let your child know that everyone makes mistakes and that you don't expect perfection. Once he has made up for his mistake, be sure to encourage self-forgiveness.

8. Use your child's mistakes as a learning experience. Once your child has taken responsibility for her behavior, talk about what she has learned from the experience.

9. Avoid becoming angry when your child makes a mistake. Anger will only reinforce your child's tendency to avoid taking responsibility because of her fear of your disapproval or wrath.

10. Make sure your child knows that you love him even when he makes a mistake. Correct the behavior without criticizing or shaming your child.

Don't say: "Admit that you did something wrong."

Do say: "Let's talk about what other choices you can make in the future and what consequences there are to each choice. That's the best thing about making mistakes—we get to learn how to do things in a new and different way!"

When your child makes excuses, have him make an "I-statement" acknowledging personal responsibility. For example, "I was late turning in my homework," or, "I didn't take out the garbage when I was supposed to." Then, have your child make a commitment—a written contract can be useful—to improve his behavior. Take away an appropriate privilege; for instance, don't allow TV for the next week or require an extra household chore until your child demonstrates improvement.

If your child persists in making excuses, first try increasing the severity of the consequences. If that doesn't work, seek professional help. Kids who consistently make excuses may be acting out feelings of perfectionism and shame. Family counseling can help define expectations and improve communication.

I will not accept excuses from my children and will hold them accountable for their actions.

SMART TIP

Make sure your child knows the difference between reasons and excuses. Reasons are explanations for how and why something occurs. Excuses are an attempt to refuse to take responsibility, usually by blaming others.

8 IF YOUR CHILD IS IRRESPONSIBLE WITH BELONGINGS

BEHAVIOR EXAMPLES

- If your child's bedroom looks like a disaster area

- If your child refuses to care for or put back personal belongings—clothing, books, toys, bicycles, etc. where they belong

- If your child mistreats, damages, or is careless with valuable items; for instance, throwing clothing on the floor, writing in books, leaving his bike in the yard, etc.

WHAT YOU CAN DO

1. Help your child arrange her bedroom and playroom in an orderly fashion.

2. Designate special places—shelves, drawers, or bins—in which your child's belongings should be stored.

3. Have your child make a list of his special things, writing next to each item exactly where and how they should be cared for and stored.

4. Have your child clean and organize her bedroom weekly. Increase her personal responsibility according to age. For example, an eight-year-old can be expected to make her bed, a twelve-year-old should clean and vacuum her own space.

5. Be a good role model by taking care of your personal belongings. For example, make sure your bedroom is neat, your car is clean, your compact discs are in their cases, etc.

6. Regularly go through your child's belongings with him, putting away or reselling those that he has outgrown or is no longer using.

7. Do not automatically replace damaged goods. Allow your child to experience the natural consequence of losing valuable belongings which she has failed to care for properly.

8. When something important is damaged and needs to be replaced, have your child pay for it or do extra household chores to help defray the cost. This also teaches the value of money.

9. Make sure your child doesn't have too many books, toys, and clothes. Too many things can be overwhelming and difficult to keep track of and care for.

10. Show your child the direct relationship between caring for and owning valuable belongings. Make this a positive statement, such as, "When you put your books in the bookcase, they stay nice and you know where to find them." Or, "Keeping your bike in the garage keeps it from being stolen or damaged by rain and snow."

Don't say: "Do you have any idea how hard I have to work to pay for these?

Do say: "Having nice things is a privilege which is earned by caring for them properly."

When your child is careless with belongings, immediately take them away. If he continues to fail to care for personal belongings, take away other valuable items. Allow your child to earn them back when he demonstrates that he can care for them.

Chronic disrespect of property is a serious behavioral problem that can escalate to vandalism and other high-risk behavior, especially during adolescence. Professional intervention by a skilled counselor is highly recommended.

I will teach my child to value all she has and I will hold her personally responsible for caring for her belongings.

SMART TIP

Have your child label his clothing, books, sporting equipment, and toys as a way of reinforcing a sense of personal ownership.

9 IF YOUR CHILD MISTREATS YOUNGER BROTHERS AND SISTERS

BEHAVIOR EXAMPLES

- If your child pushes, hits, or otherwise physically harms his siblings

- If your child teases or provokes her brothers or sisters

- If your child takes away siblings' toys or refuses to share toys, games, sports, or computer equipment with them

WHAT YOU CAN DO

1. Make a list of rules for treating family members respectfully. Post the rules in a central location in your home.

2. Discuss ways in which your child feels frustrated dealing with his siblings. Share alternate ways to deal with frustration such as using words to express feelings instead of resorting to physical violence.

3. Make sure your child has private space and her own personal belongings that are off-limits to siblings.

4. Enforce immediate consequences for any physical violence. Send your child to time-out until he can conduct himself appropriately.

5. Explain to your child how others feel when they are teased. Try to use a real-life example of a time when your child has been teased by others to reinforce how bad this feels.

6. Give your child some tangible responsibility for playing with or teaching something to her sibling, in order to cultivate the sense of self-worth that comes from being a loving family member.

7. If your child hurts one of her siblings' belongings, have her apologize and offer one of her belongings as retribution.

8. Show the importance of sharing with siblings by choosing specific books, games, or other belongings to be family property for all to share.

9. If necessary, supervise when your child is with younger siblings so that you can intervene if your child behaves inappropriately.

10. Reward your child for treating siblings respectfully. Say: "You're being very patient with your sister right now," or, "I really like it when you share your toys with your brother."

Don't say: "Be nice to your brother or else . . ."

Do say: "We are a family. This is how I expect you to treat your brothers and sisters."

If your child keeps teasing, hurting, or being mean to her siblings, use time-out as a way to isolate your child from fun family activities. If physical violence is displayed, employ more serious consequences, such as loss of privileges or extended time-out.

Kids who mistreat siblings may be acting out of frustration, jealousy, hyperactivity, or out of a need for more parental attention and supervision. If this behavior doesn't improve through time-out and loss of privileges, try to determine if your child is feeling extreme anger or frustration. In this case, a family counselor may be able to offer advice.

I will hold my child to high standards when it comes to being respectful toward his siblings so that we can have a peaceful and cooperative family life.

SMART TIP

Kids who mistreat siblings may feel competitive or in need of special attention. Encourage your child's involvement with peers by having his friends over. Have him participate in competitive sports where he can blow off steam, release energy, and interact with peers instead of siblings.

BEHAVIOR EXAMPLES

- If your child has to be pushed or reminded to finish homework on time

- If your child does a sloppy or careless job on homework assignments

- If your child does a poor job studying for tests or completing special projects

WHAT YOU CAN DO

1. Review your child's homework assignments with her on a weekly and daily basis. Some schools list homework assignments on voice mail which you and/or your child can check.

2. Set a deadline for completing each assignment. Plan for the materials and time he'll need to complete it.

3. Have your child write down all of her homework assignments in a daily planner and check off each one as it is completed.

4. Talk with your child's teachers to determine if your child is having trouble with a particular subject and needs extra help from his teacher or a tutor.

5. Make a specific time each day for your child to do homework. For example: After a snack and an hour of down-time, resting, or watching TV, it's homework time until dinner, and then a short break, before continuing until all homework is finished.

6. Be available to do homework with your child. Put aside all other activities so you can offer your child your undivided attention.

7. Remove all distractions during homework time, including music and television. Do not allow your child to talk on the phone.

8. Talk to your child to find out if he is avoiding or doing a sloppy job on homework in areas where he is having trouble understanding the material or feels incompetent or insecure. Take extra time to help your child with these subjects. Make equal time to compliment your child on homework assignments that are completed satisfactorily.

9 Create a specific work-space that is conducive for studying, including a desk, good lighting, and a comfortable chair.

10. Help your child see the positive relationship between getting homework done and self-worth. Use verbal praise, such as: "All that hard work you did studying for your science test really paid off with that B+!"

Don't say: "If you don't do better in school, you'll never amount to anything!"

Do say: "I have a lot of confidence in your ability. If you put your mind to it, you can really improve in your schoolwork!"

Remove all social privileges from your child until she finishes homework successfully and on time. Make weekend time for studying so that your child learns that schoolwork is a priority that comes before time with friends.

If your child continues to display poor study habits, set up an appointment with your child's school counselor. He or she can help you and your child set goals, get remedial assistance, and arrange for extra tutoring if necessary. One great tool is for your child to keep a journal with his teacher's help in which homework assignments are reviewed. This improves communication between your child and his teacher.

Getting homework done well and on time is an important building block for succeeding in the work force and other aspects of adult life. I will set aside the time and energy to help my child improve in this area.

SMART TIP

Poor study habits are easily reversed by cultivating organizational skills, using positive reinforcement, and rewarding your child when she shows tangible improvement.

BEHAVIOR EXAMPLES

- If your child responds rudely when you ask him to do something

- If your child continually challenges your authority

- If your child argues, debates, or negotiates when you state the rule

WHAT YOU CAN DO

1. Define respectful rules for communication with your child. For example, "If you disagree, you may ask for my reasons or state your opinion."

2. Halt the conversation any time your child is rude to you. Do not start again until she can listen and speak appropriately.

3. Explain your reason to your child once, and then refuse to negotiate further.

4. Never tolerate obscene language or verbal abuse. Enforce immediate consequences by putting your child in time-out.

5. If your child challenges you, don't defend yourself. Just calmly state your rule or expectation.

6. Be polite toward your child, spouse, and others. Kids usually speak to others the way they are spoken to at home.

7. Set a time limit for discussing your child's objections to rules. For example, say "I am willing to talk about this for three minutes." After the discussion, say: "This conversation is over."

8. Model appropriate ways to question or disagree with rules. For example, use statements such as: "I have a different opinion," or, "I'd like to say why I disagree with you."

9. Determine whether your child is learning to be rude or to talk back from peers or older kids who are impolite. You might ask, "Where did you learn to talk or behave this way?"

10. If your child is rude, don't get "hooked" into shaming, criticism, or threats. The better strategy is to review what constitutes rudeness and then provide immediate discipline, focusing on the inappropriate behavior.

Don't say: "Stop being a brat."

DON'T SAY

Do say: "I don't speak to you that way. I won't tolerate your speaking to me that way."

DO SAY

When your child is rude to you, enforce immediate consequences by taking away privileges and/or putting her in time-out. With younger kids, the loss of your attention is an effective consequence; with older kids, losing phone privileges, sports participation, school dances, or TV time may motivate them to reconsider their behavior.

SUGGESTED CONSEQUENCES

Kids who are chronically rude, talk back, or incessantly challenge authority may do so because of underlying anger or lack of respect for parents. Professional counseling can help your child get in touch with feelings of anger, and help you assert your authority so that your child doesn't feel he has to be in charge by questioning you or having the last word.

IF YOU ENCOUNTER SERIOUS RESISTANCE

I am entitled to have my child's respect.

PARENT'S AFFIRMATION

SMART TIP

Cut your child off! It's tempting to let kids express their feelings, opinions, and points-of-view *ad nauseam* in order to feel that you are open to hearing your kids out. But enough is enough! Let your child say what she wants once and then end the conversation.

BEHAVIOR EXAMPLES

· If your child constantly complains that she is fat or ugly

· If your child is a perfectionist about his school work

· If your child thinks that she is stupid or incompetent

WHAT YOU CAN DO

1. Have your child write down all of his finest qualities.

2. Tell your child that everyone makes mistakes.

3. Remind your child that effort counts more than outcome by complimenting her on how hard she tries.

4. Reinforce improvement by pointing out concrete examples of your child's efforts paying off. For example, notice that he is doing better in a certain subject or has made a new friend.

5. Be aware of your own expectations, especially ways in which you may be giving your child the message that he isn't doing as well as he should.

6. Never compare your child to her sibling or anyone else. Focus on the ways in which she is special and unique.

7. Help your child strategize ways to improve areas in which he lacks confidence, for example, eating healthier, low-fat food to control weight gain or taking a summer school course to improve his performance in a certain subject at school.

8. Be honest with your child about the ways in which you are imperfect, so that she doesn't have an overly-idealized image of you or your spouse.

9. Let your child express his feelings. Just listen without trying to convince your child that he is okay.

10. Tell your child what a blessing she is every single day.

Don't say: "That's ridiculous. Of course you're not stupid!"

Do say: "It sounds as if you feel bad about yourself. How can I help you see what a wonderful person you are?"

Being overly self-critical doesn't require negative consequences. A better strategy is to reinforce your child's strengths and help him identify areas in need of improvement.

If your child continues to be overly self-critical, professional intervention may be required in order to help build up her low self-esteem. A counselor can also assess the potential for dangerous eating disorders which are common, especially among teenage girls. Sometimes a professional counselor is more effective at helping a child see herself in a positive light. Sometimes kids feel that their parents have a skewed image of them.

I will help my child see his unique gifts and support my child in improving in areas where he lacks confidence.

SMART TIP

 Identify one area in which your child naturally excels and find ways for her to express this gift. For example, through art classes, an athletic sport, or participation in an extracurricular activity in which she can shine.

BEHAVIOR EXAMPLES

- If your child lies about not completing homework or other tasks

- If your child lies about losing or damaging personal property

- If your child lies about fighting with other kids or getting in trouble at school

WHAT YOU CAN DO

1. Never lie to your kids or others. Even "little white lies" give kids the message that lying is sometimes acceptable.

2. Call your child on his lies. Tell your child in a straightforward manner that his story isn't believable, then give him the chance to tell the truth.

3. Reassure your child that you will love her regardless of her mistakes so that she doesn't feel scared to tell you the truth. In most cases, this is why kids lie.

4. If your child lies to other people (teachers, coaches, etc.), insist that he rectify the situation with an immediate apology.

5. Explain the natural consequences of lying—other people will not believe or trust us when we lie. The story of *The Boy Who Cried Wolf* is a good tool to use.

6. Check out the facts before confronting your child with a lie.

7. Be careful not to shame your child. If she has lied, simply state the fact and the consequences.

8. Reward your child for telling the truth, especially if doing so requires taking responsibility for behavior that he knows may incur your disapproval. Use verbal praise such as, "I'm so proud of you for telling the truth," or "I know I can trust you when you tell the truth."

9. Discuss alternative ways of dealing with a situation other than lying. For instance, suggest that your child write you a note to acknowledge his responsibility in the situation, or show how he could have avoided having to lie by following the rules.

10. Be aware of whether or not your child feels threatened or intimidated, either by you or other authority figures. These feelings might motivate her to lie.

Don't say: "You're a liar."

DON'T SAY

Do say: "I don't think that you are telling the truth right now. Why don't you try it again?"

DO SAY

Developing a pattern of lying is a serious behavioral issue which should be dealt with using more severe disciplinary measures. The first time your child lies, use time-out or removal of privileges. Each subsequent lie should result in increasingly severe consequences, including grounding your child or taking away TV or phone privileges until this behavior improves.

SUGGESTED CONSEQUENCES

If disciplinary measures don't make a marked improvement in your child's behavior, seek professional help immediately. Situational lying (making up a story to cover a mistake or avoid getting into trouble in a specific situation) can escalate to chronic lying. This could include lying about involvement in high-risk behavior such as alcohol and other drug use, sexual promiscuity, and violence. A skilled therapist can identify if your child is lying because of fear of losing parental approval or peer pressure, and recommend an effective intervention.

IF YOU ENCOUNTER SERIOUS RESISTANCE

Honesty is a core element to living an integrity-filled life. I will nurture this quality by expecting honesty from my child and enforcing consequences when he doesn't tell the truth.

PARENT'S AFFIRMATION

SMART TIP

Foster open communication. Try to be as receptive and nonjudgmental as possible, so that your child will feel comfortable telling you the truth.

BEHAVIOR EXAMPLES

- If your child goes to her other parent when you say no

- If your child tries to get what he wants by making comparisons, for example, saying, "But Mom lets me stay up late," or "Dad trusts me more than you do."

- If your child tells different versions of the truth to each parent

WHAT YOU CAN DO

1. Determine mutually agreeable rules and expectations with your spouse. If you are far apart in values, beliefs, or forms of discipline, seek professional help so that you and your spouse can be as consistent as possible in your parenting.

2. Present a united front to your children by supporting each others' decisions.

3. Don't allow your child to discuss important issues unless both parents are present.

4. Don't put yourself in the position of explaining your spouse's feelings or position. Trying to arbitrate will only worsen the situation.

5. Listen to your child's feelings, but don't allow her to criticize your spouse. For example, you might say, "I hear that you are angry at Daddy, and I truly believe the two of you can work it out."

6. Be careful not to discuss your personal marital conflicts with your child. It's none of your child's concern, and he should not be in the position of taking sides.

7. Have monthly meetings where every member of the family can air their feelings and concerns with everyone present.

8. If you child approaches you with a request, find out your spouse's position prior to giving your child an answer. If necessary, say, "Dad/Mom and I will need to discuss this together before I will be ready to respond." If possible, give your child a reasonable time frame so that she knows when to expect an answer.

9. Decide with your spouse which adult is responsible for making particular decisions. For example, you will have the final word on your child's diet, your spouse will be in charge of homework, and you will make mutual decisions on manners, curfew, and safety-related issues.

10. Support each others' authority. When one spouse says, "No, you may not do that," it's essential for the other parent to stand by the decision. If you and your spouse are in disagreement, work it out in private, not in front of your kids.

Don't say: "It won't get you anywhere to play us against each other."

Do say: "Mom and Dad are a team. What one of us says goes for the other."

Cut your child off when he tries to compare you with your spouse or play you against one another. If your child tells different versions of the truth to each parent, enforce consequences similar to those for lying. Insist that your child take responsibility for having altered the truth to get what he wanted. Put him in time-out until he is ready to communicate more respectfully and responsibly.

If your child chronically plays one parent against the other, seek professional counseling for the entire family. This behavior can be seriously divisive, and may be a sign that your child is "acting out" underlying conflict between you and your spouse. A skilled professional can help you as parents to strengthen your partnership and reassert your mutual authority.

My child receives the best parenting when my spouse and I stand together in issues with our child.

SMART TIP

It's easy to feel flattered by kids seeing us as the nicer, better, or more sympathetic parent. Do your best to avoid creating alliances with your child by playing into favoritism.

15 IF YOUR CHILD IS DEMANDING

BEHAVIOR EXAMPLES

- If your child issues orders, such as "Get me a glass of milk."

- If your child demands toys, games, or other products she desires

- If your child demands your immediate and undivided attention

WHAT YOU CAN DO

1. Teach your child the appropriate way to make requests. Practice having your child say, "May I please have . . .?" or "I'd really like those high-tops I saw on TV."

2. Ignore your child when he approaches you in a demanding way. When he acts appropriately, discuss how and why your child was being demanding and why that won't get him what he wants.

3. Encourage your child to be independent. Take every possible opportunity to insist that your child do things for herself.

4. Don't jump when your child wants or needs something, unless it's a medical emergency. Teach your child that he can wait.

5. If your child demands material products, acknowledge her desire and strategize ways for her to get them. For example, you might say, "Your birthday is coming up. Let's put that video game on your wish list." Or, "If you save your allowance, you'll be able to buy that new basketball in a month."

6. Don't be demanding toward your child. Ask your child to do things in a polite and considerate way.

7. Do not give in to your child's demands, even if you are in a public situation. Remain calm and remove your child from the environment.

8. Remind your child before going into a public place (the grocery store, mall, or other peoples' homes) of the consequences of being demanding. Be prepared to leave if necessary, and follow through with this consequence.

9. Make yourself available to your child so that she doesn't feel the need to demand your attention. Let her know when you will be able to listen and talk to her about what's on her mind.

10. Before taking your child to a commercial event (a shopping mall, state fair, or movie), discuss what he will be allowed to have in the way of gifts or treats. Make it clear that there will be no further negotiation in public.

Don't say: "Stop being demanding!" This itself is a demanding statement, which may result from your own frustration and impatience with your child's behavior.

Do say: "I will not listen to demands. Please ask for what you want in a polite and respectful way."

Demanding behavior is a form of rudeness and should be treated as such. When your child is demanding, remove her from the situation until she can demonstrate respect.

Kids who continue to be demanding despite appropriate consequences may be screaming for attention or exhibiting feelings of anger and frustration. To determine whether professional intervention is required, first check with your child's teachers and other authority figures to see whether this same behavior occurs outside your home. If so, ask your child's school counselor to work with your child. If that isn't sufficient, find a family counselor to help assess your child's needs.

I will help my child learn how to ask for what he needs in a polite and respectful way. Doing so will help my child succeed in other relationships throughout his life.

SMART TIP

 Don't ever give in to your child's demands out of feelings of guilt. It's tempting to "make up" for too much time spent away from kids by indulging their demands, which will only reinforce this behavior.

16 IF YOUR CHILD IS BORED AND CAN'T ENTERTAIN HIMSELF

BEHAVIOR EXAMPLES

- If your child complains or whines that she has nothing to do

- If your child can't entertain himself without your participation

- If your child can't stick to an activity without losing interest or becoming impatient

WHAT YOU CAN DO

1. Supply your child with appropriate art supplies and other materials with which she can do creative projects.

2. Get your child started on an activity—an art project, game, or hobby, and then encourage him to finish it by himself.

3. Make a list with your child of fun and interesting things to do around the house.

4. Don't "fix" your child's boredom by immediately giving her something to do. Instead, ask: "What would you like to do?"

5. Make sure your child gets plenty of physical exercise to use up energy in a healthy way.

6. Before beginning an activity on your own, sit down with your child and plan how he is going to spend his time.

7. When your child says she is bored, assign her a household task.

8. Ask your child's teacher to provide extra-credit assignments for your child to complete at home.

9. Balance unstructured time with structured activities, such as music lessons, homework time, and play dates, so that much of his time is accounted for.

10. Encourage your child to read. There's no better activity to do alone.

Don't say: "How can you be bored? There's a million things to do around here."

Do say: "Let's make a list of five fun and interesting things for you to pick from right now."

The most effective way to counter complaints of boredom is to throw the ball back into your child's court. Encourage her to use her imagination to find something to do. Remind your child that she has the ability to be creative. If, however, your child whines or complains about her boredom, refuse to engage and put her in time-out if necessary until she can express feelings of boredom more appropriately.

Serious, ongoing problems with boredom may indicate that your child may be suffering from attention deficit disorder, may be lacking in stimulation, or need more intellectual challenge at home and/or at school. Try to discern whether your child complains of boredom when he is intellectually stimulated. A professional counselor can test your child for attention deficit disorder and recommend a course of treatment.

There's no reason for my child to be bored. I will help her find creative ways to engage her attention and imagination.

SMART TIP

Resist the temptation to resolve your child's complaints of boredom with the use of television or videos. While sticking your child in front of the TV or a video may provide a temporary solution, encouraging a passive activity will only teach your child to avoid being proactive and creative in finding constructive ways to entertain himself.

17 | IF YOUR CHILD BLAMES FAILURES ON OTHERS

BEHAVIOR EXAMPLES

- If your child says, "Johnny made me do it," when he makes a mistake

- If your child blames others for poor performance at school, for example, saying, "My teacher didn't give me the right instructions," or "Katie stole my pencil and I couldn't finish the test."

- If your child blames siblings or parents for his failure to complete household chores

WHAT YOU CAN DO

1. If your child blames someone else, check out the information to make sure of the facts before assuming that your child is to blame.

2. When your child blames others, engage her in a conversation about how the mistake or problems could have been avoided. For instance, point out, "You're blaming your teacher for giving you a poor grade, but what about the fact that you only studied a half-hour for that test?"

3. Make sure your child knows that while he may be disciplined, he is in no jeopardy of losing your love or approval by taking responsibility for his actions.

4. As soon as your child begins to blame someone else, refocus the conversation back to her by saying, "Let's talk about your part in this right now."

5. Be sure to take responsibility for your mistakes, so that your child learns not to blame others.

6. Reward your child for not blaming others. It's hard to admit blame. When your child does so, praise him by saying, "It took courage for you to admit that," or "Good for you for taking responsibility for what you did."

7. Give your child responsibilities which she can easily accomplish. This gives your child a sense of self-worth and empowerment that makes it easier to admit mistakes.

8. Help your child see how he can learn from his mistakes. Explain that mistakes give us the opportunity to learn and grow. Have your child talk about how this experience has helped him learn and grow.

9. Explain the difference between responsibility and blame. For example, if your child left her bike outside and it got stolen, she must take responsibility for having failed to take care of the bike. However, she isn't to blame for it being stolen. Make sure your child sees the relationship between irresponsibility and negative consequences.

10. Don't expect more from your child than he can reasonably deliver. If your expectations are too high, your child will have no choice but to blame others when he can't meet them.

Don't say: "It's your fault."

Do say: "It's your mistake. Let's talk about how you can solve it."

Since feelings of fear and/or shame can be the underlying cause of blaming others, give your child some time and space to feel emotionally safe before enforcing consequences. If she continues to blame others, refuse to discuss the situation and don't let your child do anything else until she is ready to take responsibility.

Blaming others is an inability to assume responsibility for one's actions. This behavioral pattern can lead to more serious problems, especially in adolescence. Kids may succumb to peer pressure and blame others for truancy, alcohol and other drug use, and other high-risk behavior. Professional counseling can help identify why your child blames others: If he feels pressured, is intimidated by authority, suffers from low self-esteem, or is engaged in activities that could endanger his safety.

Taking responsibility for mistakes is an important life skill. I will not let my child off the hook by allowing her to blame others for mistakes.

SMART TIP

It can be difficult to be objective about our own kids. Avoid falling into the trap of allowing your child to blame others because of your need to see her in a positive light. It's far more productive to hold your child accountable for her actions.

IF YOUR CHILD HAS TROUBLE ACCEPTING CRITICISM

BEHAVIOR EXAMPLES

- If your child becomes defensive when criticized

- If your child cries or becomes ashamed when she is criticized

- If your child responds to criticism by being angry or belligerent

WHAT YOU CAN DO

1. Approach your child in a loving and respectful manner. Be careful not to blame or shame him.

2. Focus on the behavior. Comment on the specific mistake or error rather than criticizing your child. For example, rather than saying, "You're lazy," say, "I see that you haven't completed your chores on time."

3. Get rid of the "Should's." Instead of saying, "You should do better," or "You should know better," say, "Here's the right way to do this."

4. Let your child know you have confidence in her ability to improve her performance or behavior.

5. Don't ever criticize your child in front of others. Take your child aside and discuss the behavior in private.

6. Try not to take your child's mistakes or failures personally. We're bound to be more critical when we feel as if our child is reflecting poorly on us.

7. Do not make fun of your child if he cries while being criticized. Stop and reassure your child that he is lovable and capable before continuing the conversation.

8. When offering constructive criticism, be sure to point out the positives as well as the negatives. For example, say, "You forgot to take out the garbage twice this week, but I also noticed that you did a really good job of getting your homework finished on time."

9. Be open to constructive criticism from your child. Parents aren't perfect. If your child learns to offer constructive criticism to you, she will be more able to accept it.

10. When you provide constructive criticism, always offer to help your child improve his behavior. Let your child know that your goal is to help him be successful in his endeavors.

Don't say: "That's not the right way to do that," or "You could do a lot better."

Do say: "Another way to do that might be . . ." or "I see you're trying. Is there anything I can do to help?"

An inability to accept constructive criticism is better dealt with by using patience and positive reinforcement than negative consequences. If your child is overly sensitive to criticism, focus on building her self-esteem. If, however, your child becomes aggressive or belligerent, stop the discussion and let your child know that you will resume talking to her when she is able to listen. If your child is crying, be sure she knows that you can help only when you can hear and understand what's being said.

Kids who have an extremely hard time accepting constructive criticism may be overreacting for a number of reasons: because they are being teased or criticized by peers, because they are comparing themselves to an unreachable idea, or because they are scared of not being able to live up to parental expectations. If this behavior persists, a kids' support group can be a great place for your child to share his feelings and learn that he isn't the only one who feels this way. He will also gain strategies for accepting constructive criticism graciously.

No one likes criticism. I will try to correct my child's flaws or failures by lovingly helping her to improve.

SMART TIP

Be aware of ways in which you may be overtly or covertly giving your child the message that his best isn't enough. If you feel as if you might be adding to your child's feelings of pressure, readjust your expectations and seek support for accepting your child as he is.

BEHAVIOR EXAMPLES

- If you child screams at friends, siblings, or parents when he is mad

- If your child uses name-calling or abusive language to express anger

- If your child throws tantrums when she doesn't get her way

WHAT YOU CAN DO

1. Teach your child alternative ways of expressing anger, using words in a respectful way.

2. Practice with your child saying, "I'm angry right now," in a calm, quiet voice.

3. Let your child know that it's perfectly okay to feel angry; it's just not okay to express it in a violent manner.

4. Don't engage with your child until his anger subsides. Say, "I will talk to you when you express yourself appropriately," or "You don't have to yell. I'm right here."

5. Don't scream or yell at your child or others. Children learn how to express anger primarily by how their parents communicate.

6. If your child uses name-calling or abusive language, enforce disciplinary measures such as time-out or loss of privileges.

7. Discuss safe ways for your child to release anger, such as hitting a pillow or using a punching bag instead of being violent toward people.

8. Don't try to deal with your child's anger if she is sick or overly-tired. Wait until your child is emotionally and physically capable of dealing with her feelings.

9. Reward your child for expressing anger appropriately. Use verbal praise, such as, "You're doing a great job describing how angry you are," or "I can really hear you and help you when you use a normal tone of voice."

10. Help your child identify when he is angry, especially how his body feels. For instance, your child may be able to recognize that his heart beats faster, fists clench, or body tightens up when angry—cues that can help him realize what he is feeling.

Don't say: "Stop that screaming right now!"

Do say: "I will listen to you when you are calm enough to talk about this."

When your child screams, yells, or uses obscenities to express anger, immediately remove her from the situation and give her a time-out to regroup. Once she is calm, resume the conversation. You may need to repeat time-out two or three times before your child is calm enough to express her anger appropriately. If your child is angry enough to hurt herself or anyone else, keep her isolated in her room until she's under control.

SUGGESTED CONSEQUENCES

Expressing anger appropriately is an acquired skill that's gained through parental role-modeling, limit-setting, and consistent enforcement of consequences. If these aren't effective in altering your child's behavior, this may be a sign that your child is experiencing a deeper level of frustration or rage that requires professional intervention. Seek help as soon as possible. Without therapeutic help, this behavior can lead to violence.

IF YOU ENCOUNTER SERIOUS RESISTANCE

I will not tolerate my child screaming or yelling at me. I will teach him how to express himself in a healthy and constructive way.

PARENT'S AFFIRMATION

SMART TIP

Try to remain calm. It's natural to react to screaming and yelling by screaming and yelling back. You might need to take a time-out to regain your composure so that you can provide calm and confident support.

BEHAVIOR EXAMPLES

- If your child keeps whining or pushing in order to get what she wants

- If your child repeatedly asks you "Why not?" when you've already said no

- If your child uses other kids to persuade you, saying, "But Billy gets to . . ."

WHAT YOU CAN DO

1. Decide where you stand before saying yes or no to your child.

2. Listen to your child's request and affirm that you have heard his feelings.

3. Have an open mind and consider whether your child's position is valid. Be willing to change your mind.

4. Consider the possibility of compromising. For example, you might say, "I am willing to let you stay up a half-hour later, but that's it."

5. Explain your reasons once and only once. Don't get pulled into extended negotiations.

6. Avoid being influenced by your child's references to what other parents allow. Once you've made a decision, have the courage of your convictions, despite how other parents might handle the situation.

7. Let your child know that if she nags or whines, the consequence will be time-out until she stops. Don't give your child your attention as long as she is whining or nagging.

8. Teach your child the relationship between nagging and negative consequences. The more he nags, pushes, or whines, the less responsive you should be.

9. Talk about positive alternatives to nagging or whining. Have your child practice asking once, asking nicely, and asking in a decent tone of voice.

10. Reward your child for not nagging. Use verbal praise, such as, "I really appreciate it when you ask me nicely," and offer tangible rewards: small gifts or added privileges so that your child learns the advantages of asking instead of nagging.

Don't say: "Stop nagging me or I'll . . ."

Do say: "I won't listen to you when you nag me. I've heard what you want and I've given you my answer."

Don't ever give in to your child's nagging or whining, no matter how beaten down you feel. If your child nags, be sure she knows that this behavior has convinced you to say "no" to her request. If nagging or whining continues, take away privileges until your child's behavior improves.

Chronic nagging or whining may indicate frustration or unmet needs that your child is unable to express. A skilled child psychologist can help your child find other, more productive ways to assert himself without nagging or whining.

No means no. I will hold my ground, even if doing so makes my child angry at me.

SMART TIP

Get earplugs. Put on loud music. Go into your bedroom and call a friend. Do whatever you need to remove yourself from your child's nagging and whining until she is ready to communicate in the right way.

SECTION THREE: AGES 13 TO 18

BEHAVIOR EXAMPLES

- If your child questions every decision you make

- If your child is regularly belligerent toward teachers, coaches, or other authority figures

- If your child accuses you of being outdated in your parenting

WHAT YOU CAN DO

1. Let your child know that you are willing to listen to her, but that ultimately, you have the final word.

2. Be very clear and specific in explaining your decisions to your child.

3. Discuss the relationship between the rules you make and your child's safety and well-being.

4. Don't engage in lengthy verbal debates. Your child will push you as far as you're willing to go.

5. Discuss alternate ways for your child to express his dissent. For example, have your child practice saying "I disagree with you," or "I feel that your decision isn't fair."

6. Give your child gradually increasing input into decision making, according to her age and maturity.

7. If your child questions your authority, turn the tables and ask him to suggest alternatives for the sake of discussion.

8. Don't allow your child's anger to alter your decision. Being firm reinforces your authority.

9. Be sure you and your spouse are in agreement on rules. Support one another in enforcing consequences. If you are a single parent, get support from a friend for remaining consistent in your rules and consequences.

10. Make sure your child knows you are taking her input into account before making a decision. Let your child know when and under what circumstances, if any, your decision may change (for example, when she is a year older, or when she demonstrates responsibility in a related area).

Don't say: "When you're the parent . . ." **DON'T SAY**

Do say: "As your parent, it is my responsibility to make decisions that keep you safe, even when you aren't happy with them." **DO SAY**

An effective way to counter your child's constant questioning of authority is to cut off the conversation. Refuse to continue the conversation until he has taken a time-out and is able to communicate respectfully. If this behavior goes on, make the natural consequences clear by taking a stronger, more authoritarian stance and allowing your child less input.

SUGGESTED CONSEQUENCES

Kids who have a serious problem respecting authority are at risk for truancy, alcohol and other drug use, violence, and getting into trouble with the law. Increase parental supervision, decrease your child's freedom, and enforce disciplinary measures such as grounding in order to reinforce the seriousness of the matter. If necessary, refuse to allow your child to socialize with other kids who are disrespectful toward authority. If none of these consequences work, consider professional counseling or a temporary stay at an adolescent group home until behavior improves.

IF YOU ENCOUNTER SERIOUS RESISTANCE

It's in my child's best interest to know that I'm in charge.

PARENT'S AFFIRMATION

SMART TIP

Never defend yourself. As the parent, you have the right to exercise your authority.

IF YOUR CHILD IS EXTREMELY VULNERABLE TO PEER PRESSURE

BEHAVIOR EXAMPLES

- If your child is easily manipulated by her friends

- If your child does things she knows are wrong in order to be popular, such as breaking rules, skipping classes, or experimenting with alcohol and other drugs

- If your child says, "But Jenny gets to do it."

WHAT YOU CAN DO

1. Teach your child to be an independent thinker. Encourage him to express his own ideas.

2. Encourage debate and dialogue in your home so that your child learns how to assert herself and stick by her own viewpoint.

3. Limit your child's involvement with friends who you feel are negative influences.

4. Encourage your child to participate in a school support group where positive peer pressure is stressed.

5. Discuss the potential dangers involved in giving in to peer pressure. Use real life examples: if possible, to point out situations in which other kids have been hurt or even killed by doing what their friends wanted them to do.

6. Reward your child whenever she refuses to be affected by peer pressure. Use verbal praise: For example, "I'm so proud of you for doing the right thing."

7. Be a good role model by not giving in to peer pressure at work or in social situations, by asserting yourself in the workplace, and by not trying to "live up to the Joneses."

8. Try to identify areas in which your child feels inadequate which may increase his susceptibility to peer pressure. For example, if your child is shy or has trouble making friends, he may be quicker to go along with the crowd.

9. Point out the privileges your child earns as a result of following your rules rather than giving in to negative peer pressure. For instance, make sure your child sees the relationship between earning your trust and having additional privileges.

10. If your child uses the "But Karen does it," line of argument to convince you to bend the rules, respond with, "I am concerned with you, not with Karen."

Don't say: "It's Karen's fault that you…"

Do say: "You're responsible for your own actions, regardless of how much pressure you feel from your friends."

Let your child know that getting into trouble, whether it results from peer pressure or not, will be met with serious consequences. When your child's behavior has clearly been influenced by peer pressure, don't allow your child to spend any more time with those friends until they can demonstrate the ability to be a positive influence. This action may motivate your child to act out, but if you truly believe a certain friend threatens your child's safety, it's worth the risk to take a tough stand. If your child continues to be overly influenced by peer pressure, take away privileges until she shows the ability to make sound, sensible choices for herself.

Kids who are overly influenced by negative peer pressure may be manifesting low self-esteem, having an identity crisis, or acting out of anger toward parents. A professional counselor can help reveal the source of your child's behavior and recommend treatment, including a support group where your child can be reinforced for thinking independently and making responsible choices.

I will nurture individuality in my child.

SMART TIP

Don't overreact. All kids this age are somewhat vulnerable to peer pressure. Assume a nonchalant attitude, but be aware of the possibility of problems.

BEHAVIOR EXAMPLES

- If your child wears torn or dirty clothing to school every day

- If your child doesn't bathe, shower, or brush her hair or teeth regularly

- If your child wears inappropriate clothing to social or public occasions

WHAT YOU CAN DO

1. Set a rule for the manner of dress that you expect for social and public outings. For instance, let your child know he is expected to dress appropriately for church/synagogue, important social events, or family holiday dinners.

2. Insist that your child wash, dry, and hang up or put away her clothing.

3. Decide the type of clothing you wouldn't want your child's grandparents to see him in, and the type of clothing that is sexually provocative, "gang attire," or other garb that projects a potentially dangerous signal.

4. Choose your battles. The older your child is, the more say she should have in choosing clothing. Don't become embattled unnecessarily.

5. Insist on good grooming, regardless of your child's personal style of dress. Clean body, hair, and teeth are health issues, which your child should be expected to respect.

6. If your child dresses inappropriately, send him back to change clothes. Don't let him leave the house until he cooperates.

7. Talk with your child about her need to follow the crowd and dress according to trends. Encourage her to express individuality by carefully thinking about what image she wants to project.

8. Take your child clothes shopping, and agree that he will choose one outfit you both find acceptable and that you will choose the other. Part of this deal is that your child will agree to wear each in appropriate settings.

9. Don't criticize your child's taste. Even if you find her style ugly or unflattering, criticism will merely add fuel to the fire.

10. Compliment your child when he looks clean and neat.

Don't say: "The way you look embarrasses me."

Do say: "For this occasion, you will need to change your clothing."

If your child is dirty, disheveled, or inappropriately dressed, give her ten minutes to wash and change clothing. If she refuses, take away phone or TV privileges or enforce grounding until your child cleans up her act.

SUGGESTED CONSEQUENCES

If your child persists in being unclean or slovenly, don't allow him to socialize at all until this behavior improves. If your child continues to wear clothing that sends a sexual or violent message, seek professional intervention to determine whether your child is in danger or simply making a harmless or trendy fashion statement.

IF YOU ENCOUNTER SERIOUS RESISTANCE

My child is not a reflection of me. I will allow my child to express her personal style as long as she is relatively neat and clean.

PARENT'S AFFIRMATION

SMART TIP

Find old photographs of yourself as a teenager. Seeing how you dressed then can help give you perspective.

BEHAVIOR EXAMPLES

- If your child gives you one-word answers to questions

- If your child turns you off when you try to talk to him about what's going on at school, work, or with friends

- If your child is sullen and unapproachable

WHAT YOU CAN DO

1. Talk to your child whether or not she responds. For example, share something interesting about your day or comment on what's going on in the news so she can just listen without having to interact.

2. Ask your child if something is bothering him. Let your child know that you are ready to listen whenever he is ready.

3. Suggest that your child write you a note or letter instead of talking to you.

4. Encourage your child to talk to her friends about what's going on. Kids appreciate it when parents understand the importance of peer support.

5. Never threaten your child with negative consequences for failure to communicate.

6. Ask your child's school counselor to talk to your child to determine whether or not there is something he is hiding or struggling to resolve.

7. Ask your child if there is another adult—a teacher, coach, or close relative—whom she might want to talk with.

8. Don't inundate your child with questions. Kids sometimes stop talking because they are afraid that they don't have the "right" answer.

9. Reassure your child that you won't judge him and that you can be trusted with confidences. You might say, "I'm here for you and I promise that whatever you say will stay between you and me."

10. Find out if your child is angry about something you have done. Teenagers may stop talking as a way to "get back" at parents.

Don't say: "You'd better talk to me right now, or else . . ."

Do say: "If it helps to talk, know that I'm here for you."

Many teenagers go through a stage during which they are highly uncommunicative. Although this is frustrating for parents, your child should be allowed her silence, with this exception: It's not okay to be rude, e.g., refusing to answer when spoken to. Rudeness, as always, should result in negative consequences, such as time-out or loss of privileges.

SUGGESTED CONSEQUENCES

If you feel that your child's lack of communication indicates that he is having serious problems, seek professional help. Kids who shut down may be experiencing clinical depression and might require counseling or medication. If your child has stopped talking because he is angry or scared of telling you what's really going on, this, too, can be addressed by a skilled adolescent therapist.

IF YOU ENCOUNTER SERIOUS RESISTANCE

I will take my cues from my child unless I feel that her silence reflects problems that need professional intervention.

PARENT'S AFFIRMATION

SMART TIP

Teenagers are terribly sensitive to feeling intruded upon by parents. Be aware of how you phrase questions, taking care to not push your child to divulge more personal information than he is comfortable sharing.

BEHAVIOR EXAMPLES

- If your child tells you or other people to shut up

- If your child uses swear words or obscene gestures

- If your child says, "Gimme or Get me that . . ." instead of saying please and thank you

WHAT YOU CAN DO

1. Define rudeness for your child. Make a list of rude behavior such as swearing, demanding, interrupting, etc. and post it in your child's bedroom.

2. Establish consequences for rudeness. Make sure your child knows that every incident of rudeness will be immediately punished.

3. Discuss alternatives to rudeness. For instance, if your child interrupts, after enforcing consequences, have your child practice saying, "I'd like to have a turn to talk now."

4. Find out if your child is angry or frustrated. The inability to deal with and express difficult feelings can often be the cause of rudeness.

5. Help your child express his anger or frustration in a more constructive way, such as taking a time-out, hitting a pillow, or asking for help.

6. Never swear in front of your children. Kids imitate their parents if they get the message that obscenity is acceptable for adults.

7. If your child is rude in public, remove her immediately and enforce consequences, even if doing so means going home and sending your child to her room.

8. Insist that your child apologize for rude behavior, both to you and to others.

9. Have your child make a list of alternative words to swearing, such as "Oh, shoot!" or, "Bummer!" Although swearing has always been popular among teenagers, there are other "cool" terms that can replace four-letter words.

10. Limit your child's social interaction with other kids who are rude or use obscene language or gestures. Kids this age are prone to imitate peers in order to gain acceptance and approval.

Don't say: "How dare you speak to me that way?!"

Do say: "Rudeness won't be tolerated in our home."

Anytime your child is rude, enforce immediate consequences by walking away or, if physically possible, remove him from the situation. Refuse to interact with your child until he has apologized and has demonstrated the ability to conduct himself properly. If rudeness continues, begin taking away privileges until your child's behavior improves.

SUGGESTED CONSEQUENCES

If your child is continually rude in a variety of settings (home, school, social situations), a skilled family counselor can help her sort out feelings of anger and frustration and learn how to express them appropriately.

IF YOU ENCOUNTER SERIOUS RESISTANCE

There is no excuse for rudeness. Period.

PARENT'S AFFIRMATION

SMART TIP

Don't act shocked when your child is rude. Often, rudeness is caused by your child's need for attention. Rewarding rudeness with attention (acting shocked or overreacting) will reinforce this behavior. Instead, remain calm and unruffled as you enforce consequences.

BEHAVIOR EXAMPLES

- If your child skips classes or breaks rules at school

- If your child violates curfew, abuses phone privileges, or breaks other rules at home

- If your child doesn't follow rules in public places, e.g., throwing popcorn in movie theatres, ignoring the lifeguard at the swimming pool, etc.

WHAT YOU CAN DO

1. Make sure your child understands the rules at home. Expect your child to occasionally break them, as pushing limits is a normal part of adolescence.

2. Explain the rules to your child so that she understands why they're necessary. For example, "Calling home when you go somewhere assures me that you are safe," or "Skipping classes will result in a failing grade."

3. Describe the direct relationship between breaking rules and natural consequences. For example, "If you don't call when you arrive somewhere, I won't know that you are safe, in which case, you will not be allowed to go out." Or "If you skip classes and fail science, you will be required to go to summer school instead of going to camp."

4. Create a written contract with your child in which she agrees to follow certain rules. For example, "I, Julie, agree to be home by 10:00 on weekends. If I am going to be late, I will call home and let my parents know."

5. Reward your child for following the rules using verbal praise such as, "I really appreciate it when you call and let me know where you are," or with increased privileges. Have your child write down the rules and circle ones that are broken in order to keep track of his performance.

6. Allow your child to experience natural consequences when she breaks rules outside the home. Don't rescue your child or intervene in order to lessen the consequences.

7. If your child breaks rules at school, meet with his teachers, school counselor, and principal. Work together to decide on and enforce consequences.

8. Let your child express her feelings about the rules. If your child feels a certain rule is unfair, try to be open to her point of view, and unless safety is involved, consider a compromise.

9. Ask your child to tell you what rules he would make if he were the parent. This exercise gives your child the chance to express himself, while having to consider the responsibilities involved in parenting.

10. Make family rules that apply to all members and follow them yourself. For example, agree that no member of the family is allowed to do anything else until his room is clean.

DON'T SAY

Don't say: "You're bad. You've broken another rule." (This criticizes the person instead of the behavior.)

DO SAY

Do say: "Talking on the phone after nine o'clock is a violation of the rules."

SUGGESTED CONSEQUENCES

Every rule you establish should be accompanied by a concrete consequences set ahead of time. Consequences should be closely related to the violation whenever possible; for example, breaking curfew should result in having to stay home at night, skipping class should be disciplined by having to remain after school, etc.

IF YOU ENCOUNTER SERIOUS RESISTANCE

A pattern of rule-breaking can lead to increasingly serious infractions such as vandalism, theft, and other illegal behavior. If appropriate consequences aren't sufficient to keep your child from breaking rules at home, school, and other public places, seek professional intervention at once. A short-term adolescent treatment program may be required for your child to reverse this potentially destructive pattern of behavior.

PARENT'S AFFIRMATION

Following rules is another basic life skill that my child will need to survive and succeed in the world. I will be firm and consistent in expecting my child to follow the rules.

SMART TIP

Be consistent. Except in special circumstances, be absolutely clear in establishing rules and unwavering in enforcing them.

IF YOUR CHILD TRIES TO GET WHAT HE WANTS BY COMPARING YOU TO OTHER PARENTS

BEHAVIOR EXAMPLES

- If your child says, "Nick's mother lets him."

- If your child says how much nicer, more permissive, and understanding her friends' parents are

- If your child envies other kids because their parents are in a higher economic bracket

WHAT YOU CAN DO

1. Don't be intimidated by comparisons with other parents, especially in the area of permissiveness. Know your values, and set limits accordingly.

2. If your child says: "Betsy's mom lets her . . ." don't respond at all. You needn't defend your rules or parenting style.

3. Try to listen undefensively if your child raves about another parent. Your child may be trying to communicate her need for more time, attention, or empathy from you.

4. Ask your child how you're doing as his or her parent. Be open to ways in which you might be willing to improve or modify your parenting.

5. Encourage your child to entertain his friends at your home. He may be surprised at his friends' positive perceptions of you.

6. Don't feel pressured by other parents' ability to provide greater material comforts. Comments such as, "Kim's parents got her new skis for Christmas," should be responded to firmly and swiftly by saying, "Mom/Dad and I are doing our best to provide for you. If you want skis, here are a few ideas for how you can work toward earning the money."

7. Join a parenting support group in which you can share your feelings, listen to other parents discuss their frustrations, and gain encouragement for doing your best.

8. Have your child name three or four things he likes about the way you parent and the sorts of privileges he gets in your family.

9. Don't compare your child to other kids. Treat her as a unique individual so that she can learn to do the same with you and your spouse.

10. Talk with your child about diversity. Expose him to individuals from all walks of life.

Don't say: "If you don't like it here, why don't you go live at Susie's house?"

Do say: "I'm your Mom/Dad and it's up to me to decide what's safe and appropriate for you to do and have."

If your child compares your economic status with that of other parents, remind her of what she has. If your child uses comparisons with other parents to try and get you to be more permissive, tell her that this argument will result in consequences if it continues.

If your child persists, be less permissive, withdrawing a privilege or limiting her freedom to come and go as she pleases.

I'm proud of how I am raising my child.

SMART TIP

Take your child to a homeless shelter or have him volunteer at a food shelf in order to gain perspective and gratitude.

BEHAVIOR EXAMPLES

- If your child doesn't study or turn in homework assignments on time

- If your child is performing below his academic ability

- If your child has a poor attitude in the classroom

WHAT YOU CAN DO

1. Go over assignments with your child on a daily and weekly basis.

2. Determine with your child how much time each assignment will require and what tools and materials are needed (computer, calculator, art supplies, etc.).

3. Supervise your child's homework and go over each assignment as it is completed. Offer to help by typing or participating in a project.

4. Set regular study hours for your child and don't allow her to watch TV or use the telephone until all homework is completed.

5. Determine whether your child is struggling with certain academic subjects. Make an appointment to meet with your child and his teacher to get extra help. Having your child and his teacher keep a journal of academic progress is a useful tool.

6. Don't accept any excuses for poor grades in school. Make sure your child sees the direct relationship between studying and academic performance.

7. Reinforce academic success in areas where your child does well as a way to build confidence and self-esteem.

8. Set academic goals with your child and reward success with agreed-upon incentives, such as a special book, computer game, or social activity with friends.

9. Ask your child's teacher for ideas on how to improve your child's attitude; for example, physically separating her from "troublemakers" or putting your child in charge of a special project in which she can shine.

10. Reinforce the positive relationship between studying and satisfaction. When your child works hard on a homework assignment or does well on a quiz, ask him to notice personal feelings of pride. Celebrate achievements with a special outing to a sports event, movie, or shopping trip.

Don't say: "If you don't work harder in school, you'll never amount to anything."

Do say: "You're very bright and capable when you put your best effort forward."

Reinforce the fact that doing well in school is a priority by enforcing consequences for lack of effort, sloppy work, or poor study habits. If your child isn't trying or is producing work beneath her abilities, limit all social activities until schoolwork improves. You might also enroll your child in a class for developing good study habits, which may be available through summer school curriculum.

SUGGESTED CONSEQUENCES

If your child continues to do poorly in school, consult a psychologist who specializes in learning disorders to determine if your child is dyslexic or has any other impairment. School psychologists can also work with your child to determine his personal learning style. For instance, some kids become extremely anxious during tests. If this is the case, talk to the child's teachers to see if tests can be given orally. If a bad attitude is the primary issue, have a psychologist explore areas of anger or frustration that may be contributing to your child's poor performance. Underachievement is often a manifestation of perfectionism, which can also be addressed by a skilled therapist.

IF YOU ENCOUNTER SERIOUS RESISTANCE

There are many ways to help my child improve her academic performance. I will contribute my time and energy in any way I can, and I will seek outside resources if necessary.

PARENT'S AFFIRMATION

SMART TIP

Reward small signs of improvement. Be sure your child knows that any effort in the right direction is worthy of praise.

⑨ IF YOUR CHILD WON'T PARTICIPATE IN FAMILY ACTIVITIES

BEHAVIOR EXAMPLES

- If your child wants to eat in front of the TV or in the bedroom instead of with the family

- If your child refuses to attend family gatherings such as Thanksgiving or Easter

- If your child doesn't want to attend church or go on other family outings

WHAT YOU CAN DO

1. Specify what is and isn't mandatory for your child to participate in. For example, you might agree that your child must eat dinner with the family, but doesn't have to come to the neighborhood block party.

2. Ask your child why she doesn't want to participate. Some family outings may be boring or unnecessary for a teenager to attend.

3. Invite your child to suggest family activities he would enjoy. Make sure to follow through on a few of his suggestions.

4. Allow your child to invite a friend to share in family activities. Many teenagers are more willing to participate when a peer is included.

5. If a family event is mandatory, let your child know how long she will be expected to participate. Don't say, "We'll be at Grandma's for an hour," and then stay three hours.

6. Encourage your child to bring homework, a book, or video when you attend family gatherings that are likely to last several hours.

7. Try to have some extended family gatherings at your home so that your child can participate for awhile and then spend some time doing other things in her own room.

8. Reinforce a respect for the elderly. Make sure that your child understands the importance of spending time with grandparents who will not be around forever.

9. Don't insist that your child sit with you at church or other family events. Allow her to sit with friends or relatives her own age as long as she participates.

10. Make family events as enjoyable as possible by keeping conflict to a minimum. Kids whose parents fight or are on shaky ground with their own parents or other relatives are unlikely to want to participate in family gatherings.

Don't say: "You'll go wherever I tell you."

Do say: "You're a member of this family and this is one of those times when I expect you to participate."

If your child argues or creates a scene about participating in family events, enforce a consequence such as losing phone privileges or not being able to spend time with friends. If your child outright refuses to attend a family event, go anyway, and ground her for refusing to participate.

Most teenagers go through a stage during which they would prefer to not spend time in family activities. Don't panic if your child argues about going to family dinners or social gatherings as long as he complies with bottom-line expectations, such as participating in Christmas, Easter, Hanukkah, weddings, funerals, and other significant life-cycle events. If, however, your child continues to be antisocial across the board or at every family event, enforce increasingly severe consequences until he complies.

I will let go of expecting my child to participate in every family activity, but I will firmly expect her attendance at mandatory events.

SMART TIP

 This has nothing to do with you! It's the rare teenager who chooses family time over time with friends.

BEHAVIOR EXAMPLES

- If your child lies about where he is, has been, or is going

- If your child lies about how she is doing in school

- If your child lies about doing things he knows are against the rules, such as skipping school, shoplifting, or using alcohol and other drugs

WHAT YOU CAN DO

1. Reassure your child that nothing she does, even if it incurs consequences, will diminish your love.

2. Check out the facts before confronting your child with a lie.

3. Comment on the behavior (e.g., "I called Todd's house and you weren't there.") rather than making accusations (e.g., "You're lying to me.")

4. Be aware of your child's whereabouts. Make sure that he checks in by phone regularly.

5. Know your child's friends and their parents. Being in "the loop" decreases your child's ability to con you.

6. Talk to your child's teachers often so that you can verify whether your child is giving you an accurate report of her performance.

7. Make sure your child understands the relationship between lying and negative consequences. All dishonesty should be punished by loss of freedom so that your child sees the importance of earning trust.

8. Encourage your child to let you know if he is afraid to tell you anything. Be as approachable and nonjudgmental as possible.

9. Discuss imaginary scenarios with your child in which she asks: "Would you be mad at me if I . . . ?" or "Would I get in trouble if I . . . ?" This exercise opens discussion of potential "trouble areas" that your child may be prone to lie about, especially if she is afraid of your reaction.

10. Let your child know that lying compounds problems. If he lies about doing something wrong, double the consequence so that he realizes that lying has made the problem that much worse.

Don't say: "I'll never trust you again . . . "

Do say: "I want to be able to trust you. Being honest is one way to earn my trust."

Every incident of lying should be punished by immediately confronting the behavior, taking away a privilege, and having your child apologize. After enforcing the consequence, engage your child in an honest discussion of why she lied and be sure she understands the natural consequences of lying (e.g., loss of friends, being fired at work, etc.)

Professional intervention should be used in order to correct lying before it becomes a serious and chronic behavioral pattern. A skilled adolescent therapist can assess whether your child is lying about dangerous or self-destructive behavior and determine a course of treatment.

Honesty is a core element of helping my child develop integrity.

SMART TIP

Don't excuse lying under any circumstances, even if your child lies in order to prevent hurting someone's feelings. Make sure your child knows that honesty is the best policy.

BEHAVIOR EXAMPLES

- If your child is spending time with kids who lie, cheat, or steal

- If your child is hanging out with kids who are using alcohol and other drugs

- If your child is involved with kids who constantly get in trouble at home or at school

WHAT YOU CAN DO

1. Have your child invite his new friends to your house so that you can observe their attitudes and behavior. If your child refuses to have a specific friend over, this can indicate that he knows this friend isn't acceptable.

2. Don't criticize your child's friends. Simply comment on behavior you disapprove of.

3. Explain your reasons for disapproving of certain friends. Reinforce your concern for your child's safety and security.

4. Don't forbid your child to hang out with a certain crowd of kids. Rather, make an informed decision about each individual child involved.

5. Encourage your child to maintain or renew ties with old friends.

6. Tighten the reins. Limit her freedom so that she has less opportunity to get into trouble. For example, enforce a stiffer curfew or forbid your child to hang out at the mall or other places where her new friends congregate.

7. Be careful to not base your judgments on your child's new friends' appearances. Focus only on behavior that is unsafe or inappropriate.

8. Allow your child to experience the natural consequences of hanging out with the wrong crowd, e.g., getting into trouble, losing other friends, etc. Be sure to emphasize that you are there for your child always—especially in times of trouble.

9. Calmly point out the changes in your child's attitude or behavior since spending time with these particular kids.

10. Encourage your child to speak up and defend his personal values. Reinforcing your child's individuality helps him to make sound, sensible choices.

Don't say: "Those kids are bad news."

Do say: "I don't want you to spend time with _____ because he or she _____.

Forbidding your child to associate with kids who have a bad track record can easily backfire. Kids often dig their heels in harder in the face of parental disapproval. However, your child is likely to experience a variety of natural negative consequences by hanging out with the wrong crowd, such as succumbing to peer pressure, getting in trouble, or losing the respect of others. Unfortunately, your child may need to experience these sorts of consequences in order to reexamine her choice of friends.

If your child continues to hang out with the wrong crowd, especially in the case of gangs, you might consider extreme measures, such as grounding your child from any social activity and/or moving your child to another school. Counseling can also help your child be less susceptible to peer pressure and more discerning about whom he associates with.

It's my responsibility to ensure my child's safety in every possible way.

SMART TIP

Don't exaggerate in order to convince your child that his or her friends are bad influences. Stick to the facts.

12 IF YOUR CHILD WON'T HELP AROUND THE HOUSE

BEHAVIOR EXAMPLES

- If your child won't do her chores

- If your child doesn't clean up after his messes

- If your child complains when you ask her to help

WHAT YOU CAN DO

1. Make a list of all available household chores and ask your child to choose three or four that he will be responsible for.

2. Make a family list of rules and responsibilities that every member of the family must respect. For example, every member of the family, including young children, can be expected to clear their plates and put away their belongings.

3. Don't allow your child to do anything else until her chores are done.

4. Give your child an allowance or privileges based on fulfilling his responsibilities around the house.

5. Set aside specific times for specific tasks to be accomplished. For example, have your child take out the garbage right after school, so that she is used to a certain routine.

6. Make chores fun by having the family do them together, followed by a special treat, such as a video or dinner out at a restaurant.

7. Make sure that your child is aware of all the work you do both within and outside of the home. Don't allow your child to assume that "things just get done."

8. Reinforce the relationship between helping around the house and enjoying privileges. When your child finishes a task, reward him with verbal praise, such as: "You did a great job vacuuming the living room." Or allow your child to do something he enjoys.

9. Ask your child to do something only once. Don't explain; don't negotiate.

10. Acknowledge all positive contributions your child makes. Let her know that your family runs more smoothly when everyone does their part.

Don't say: "You're a spoiled brat. You never do anything around here to help."

DON'T SAY

Do say: "I expect you to do your share."

DO SAY

If your child complains about or refuses to help around the house, withdraw privileges until he cooperates. If this behavior continues, increase your child's chores. The more he complains or refuses to help, the more tasks he should be given.

SUGGESTED CONSEQUENCES

If your child doesn't respond to the consequences above, severely limit her freedom and privileges. Don't allow your child to do anything other than go to school and attend other mandatory activities until she demonstrates both an improved attitude and a willingness to assume full responsibility for her share of household tasks.

IF YOU ENCOUNTER SERIOUS RESISTANCE

I already do enough. I should expect my children to lend a hand.

PARENT'S AFFIRMATION

SMART TIP

Don't do your child's household chores for him. If necessary, offer to do them with your child.

BEHAVIOR EXAMPLES

- If your child cheats at school (copying homework or cheating on tests)

- If your child cheats while playing games with friends

- If your child is a sore loser

WHAT YOU CAN DO

1. Try to find out why your child has cheated. For example, he may be afraid of disappointing you by getting a poor grade in one of his classes. Help your child set realistic and attainable goals.

2. Encourage cooperation rather than competition. Many sports activities, such as basketball, football, soccer, and team bowling emphasize team effort rather than individual success. Create family activities in which each member participates without anyone winning or losing.

3. Praise your child for making an effort. Let her know that trying hard is more important than getting a good grade or winning a game.

4. Have realistic expectations based on your child's abilities. Don't give him the message that you expect more than he can deliver.

5. Rather than always letting your child win so that she will feel good, occasionally let your child lose fairly when you are playing a game.

6. Encourage your child to talk about how he feels when he doesn't get the highest grade or win at a game. Discuss alternate ways to deal with feelings of disappointment, such as saying, "I am sad that I didn't do better," or making a commitment to try harder the next time around.

7. Be honest about your areas of weakness so that your child doesn't have an inflated image of you which she tries to live up to.

8. Explain to your child why cheating is wrong. Allow him to experience the natural consequences of cheating (e.g., receiving a failing grade, losing friends, etc.).

9. Be a good role model. Don't cheat. Avoid cheating even in small, seemingly insignificant ways such as cutting in front of others in traffic or looking for loopholes in filing taxes. Any and all examples of cheating, however trivial, will be interpreted as acceptance of this behavior.

10. Take your child aside when reprimanding her for cheating. Shaming her, particularly in public, won't build character, it will only humiliate your child.

Don't say: "You're a cheater."

Do say: "It's not okay to cheat. Let's talk about what you could have done instead."

All incidents of cheating should be dealt with by withdrawing a privilege. If your child cheats at school, meet with her teacher and agree on appropriate consequences such as detention or having to do extra homework assignments.

If your child continues to cheat both at home and outside the home (at school, work, or in social situations), have a professional assess whether your child is suffering from extreme insecurity and dangerously low self-esteem. Have your child work with a therapist on a regular basis to build confidence and self-acceptance.

I will remind my child that his best is good enough.

SMART TIP

Kids cheat when they don't believe their best is good enough. Try to identify areas in which your child feels deficient and work on ways to improve her confidence.

BEHAVIOR EXAMPLES

- If your child is always looking at herself in the mirror

- If your child constantly changes outfits or spends (or asks you to spend) too much money on clothing

- If your child can't stop complaining about his hair, weight, complexion, or other physical qualities

WHAT YOU CAN DO

1. Help your child focus on other aspects of himself, such as talent, intelligence, or mastery of various skills.

2. Limit your child's time spent staring at the television or looking at fashion magazines.

3. Be aware of how much attention you pay to your own appearance so that your child doesn't get the impression that looks are overly-important.

4. Make a conscious effort to play-down your child's physical appearance. When she looks nice, compliment her only once. When she appears sloppy, unkempt, or wears unflattering apparel, look the other way unless your child is going out in public. In that case, simply ask her to clean up or change clothes.

5. If your child complains of being overweight, encourage him to eat healthy, nutritious food rather than going on a strict diet.

6. Make sure your child gets plenty of exercise. Working out or participating in athletic activities strengthens your child's body and improves his self-esteem.

7. Don't buy or allow your child to buy excessive amounts of new clothing. Reinforce the idea that a positive body image comes from within, not from what you wear.

8. If your child complains of a reasonable problem with his appearance (being overweight despite following a low-fat diet or having a serious case of pimples that won't go away), take him to a doctor who can recommend treatment.

9. Don't spend hours getting dressed or spend lots of money on cosmetics. This gives your child the message that looks are extremely important and worthy of investment.

10. Help your child appreciate her own unique beauty. Point out particular innate physical qualities that enhance her appearance.

Don't say: "It doesn't matter how you look."

DON'T SAY

Do say: "You have many fine qualities including your appearance."

DO SAY

Being obsessed with appearance should be handled with positive reinforcement and refocusing of your child's priorities rather than by enforcing negative consequences. Excessive concern with appearance stems from insecurity, in which case, punishing your child may result in his cutting off communication and/or feeling worse about himself.

SUGGESTED CONSEQUENCES

It's natural for teenagers, especially girls, to be extremely focused on their appearance. If, however, your child can't stop being obsessed with her looks, a support group can be a useful resource. Sharing similar concerns and getting feedback from other teenagers can help your child be more accepting of her appearance.

IF YOU ENCOUNTER SERIOUS RESISTANCE

I will try my best to help my child accept how she looks.

PARENT'S AFFIRMATION

SMART TIP

Make sure your child is involved in interesting and stimulating activities so that he has less time to think about his looks.

BEHAVIOR EXAMPLES

- If your child is overly possessive about his belongings

- If your child seems oblivious to others peoples' feelings

- If your child needs to be the center of attention

WHAT YOU CAN DO

1. Make sure your child has certain material objects that belong solely to her.

2. Designate certain material possessions as communal property that family members must share (the TV, the phone, the computer, etc.).

3. Take turns talking and listening during dinner and other family gatherings so that your child doesn't monopolize the conversation.

4. Encourage giving in your family, whether it's through the exchange of hugs, gifts, or warm words of encouragement.

5. Make charitable giving a family tradition. Discuss charitable contributions openly with your children and encourage them to make small contributions, even if it's only a dollar. The objective is to teach your child that giving feels good.

6. Expose your child to the real world. Don't shelter your child from poverty, hunger, or homelessness; rather, discuss the plight of those in need and share ideas of how to help.

7. Reward your child for thoughtfulness or generosity with verbal praise. Do not reward generosity with material gifts which might give your child the message that they are being "paid" to share what they have.

8. When your child acts selfishly, find out if he is feeling bad about anything. People (including adults) are more prone to act selfishly when they are feeling scared, angry, or self-protective.

9. Be a good model by demonstrating generosity. Give freely of yourself to your partner, your child, and those around you.

10. Take time as a family to give thanks for all you have. Talk with your child about appreciation for necessities, comforts, and most of all, each other.

Don't say: "Stop being so selfish."

Do say: "There is plenty of (time, money, attention) to go around."

When your child acts selfishly, impose a time-out for the express purpose of self-reflection. Discuss your child's selfish behavior. (Remember: comment on the act, not on the person. For instance, say: "It was selfish of you to refuse to give your sister a bite of your candy bar," not, "You're a selfish person.") If your child is overly-possessive of her belongings, take a valued possession away until she is ready to share. If your child lacks empathy or compassion, have her do volunteer work in order to realize how fortunate she is.

If the consequences are ineffective in helping your child be less selfish and more aware of others, a professional assessment might be useful in determining underlying causes. Unresolved fear, anger, or frustration may be at the roots of this behavior.

I will help my child to experience a sense of gratitude and abundance.

SMART TIP

Acting selfishly does not mean that your child is a bad person. It simply means he is afraid that there is a scarcity of resources (time, energy, material objects, or, in many cases, love).

NOTES